FAT QUARTER
HOME

25 projects to make from short lengths of fabric

Amanda Russell & Juliet Bawden

First published 2017 by
Guild of Master Craftsman Publications Ltd
Castle Place, 166 High Street, Lewes,
East Sussex, BN7 1XU

Text © Amanda Russell and Juliet Bawden, 2017
Copyright in the Work © GMC Publications Ltd, 2017

ISBN 978 1 78494 385 1

While every effort has been made to obtain permission from the copyright holders for all material used in this book, the publishers will be pleased to hear from anyone who has not been appropriately acknowledged and to make the correction in future reprints.

The publishers and author can accept no legal responsibility for any consequences arising from the application of information, advice or instructions given in this publication.

A catalogue record for this book is available from the British Library.

Publisher Jonathan Bailey
Production Manager Jim Bulley
Senior Project Editor Sara Harper
Editor Cath Senker
Managing Art Editor Gilda Pacitti
Art Editor Luana Gobbo
Photographer Rowland Roques-O'Neil
Step photography Studio of R&B Designs
Picture credit Cover illustrations: Shutterstock/Ohn Mar

Colour origination by GMC Reprographics
Printed and bound in Turkey

A note on measurements
The imperial measurements in these projects are converted from metric. While every attempt has been made to ensure that they are as accurate as possible, some rounding up or down has been inevitable. For this reason, it is always best to stick to one system or the other throughout a project: do not mix metric and imperial units.

CONTENTS

INTRODUCTION

Both of us have always enjoyed sewing, and from an early age we were making clothes for dolls and teddies. We soon progressed to household items and gifts for family and friends, and from there to making our own clothes for everyday and special occasions. If, like us, you are addicted to creating, then you are bound to have a stash of fabric in glorious patterns and colours just waiting to be used. There are always remnants left over from projects, as well as those must-have, impulse-buy fat quarters of fabrics you spot when you're out and about. In this book we've designed 25 fabulous projects that will help you transform these oddments into gorgeous items for your home. And nowadays with the emphasis on looking after the environment, it's also immensely rewarding to feel that you're helping to make the most of resources while creating something lovely from leftover bits and pieces.

Projects are organized according to different parts of your home: the kitchen/diner, utility room, bedroom, bathroom and sitting room. They range from a quick and cost-effective update of an old chair, to practical but pretty storage solutions, with customized bed linen, cushion covers and lots of other useful and decorative items in between. Each project can either be made from fat quarters, or from remnants pieced together. A fat quarter is simply half a yard of fabric cut in half again vertically, and in this book it refers to an 18 x 22in (46 x 56cm) maximum piece of fabric. Sizes do vary, depending upon the width from which the fabric is cut, so bear this in mind when working out your fabric requirements.

Most of the projects are very easy, with simple instructions and step-by-step images to help you on your way, and to make them you will only need basic sewing skills and a sewing machine. We hope you have as much fun making them as we did.

Amanda and Juliet

THE BASICS

MATERIALS AND EQUIPMENT

We like to keep things simple, so our list of essential tools mostly consists of items you will already have. For a few projects you will need additional equipment, such as a staple gun for the drop-in seat.

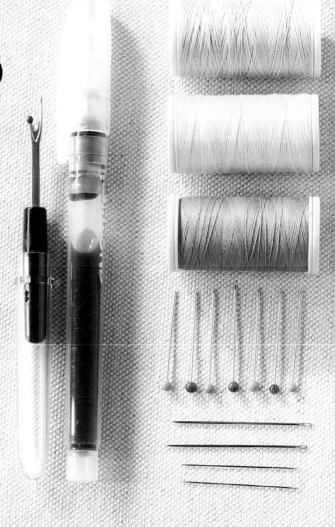

SCISSORS A large pair of dress-making scissors for cutting fabric and a smaller pair for detailed tasks, such as cutting threads, are a must. Keep a different pair for cutting paper, because this blunts scissors. Label your scissors so you know which is which!

SEAM RIPPER This handy tool is essential for easy unpicking if you need to correct any mistakes in your sewing.

PINS Glass-headed pins are the best to use. With their bold colours, they are visible, easy to pick up, a good length and will pierce fabric readily.

NEEDLES Ensure you have a selection of small and large needles, as well as thicker embroidery needles, for hand sewing.

TAPE MEASURE AND RULER Nothing beats a dress-making tape measure with both metric and imperial measurements. A ruler is useful for smaller jobs.

SEWING MACHINE A sewing machine that does straight stitching and zigzag is essential for the projects. Along with a straight stitch sewing foot, you will need a zipper foot. Store your sewing machine in its case and, to keep it performing well, have it serviced regularly. Sharp needles are a must, so keep a stash and, when you start a project, replace the existing needle with one the correct width for the fabric you are using.

PENS, PENCILS AND TRACING PAPER A water-erasable pen is essential for marking fabric. It is really simple to use and you can remove the marks later with a burst of steam while ironing. Have pens, pencils and tracing paper ready for drawing patterns. You can also use baking parchment to make patterns.

IRON AND IRONING BOARD
Buy the best steam iron you can afford. It makes all the difference to the finish of a project to iron as you go along, ironing after each step you have completed. Your ironing board should be firm and stable with a clean, well-padded cover.

SAFETY PINS Use safety pins for threading elastic and ribbon, and for turning loops of fabric the right way out.

EMBROIDERY HOOP This is essential for stretching fabric to keep it stable while you are embellishing it with stitching.

ZIPS These often used to be covered to form a discreet and hidden way of creating an opening. Now zips are often used to visually lift a project by adding one in a contrasting colour. You can buy zips online in bulk; this is cost-effective especially if you're repeating a project for multiple gifts.

FABRICS You can often buy ends of rolls and remnants of designer fabrics for a fraction of their original price. Most fabrics are suitable for the projects in this book; these have been made up in cotton fabric. You can mix and match oddments to make up different lengths. Always prewash fabric to avoid problems with shrinking later.

INTERFACING If the fabric for a project needs to be thicker and more substantial, iron fusible interfacing or fleece to the reverse side.

THREAD Cotton thread is strong and firm, and comes in a rainbow of colours. A neutral colour is useful as it can be used for different projects. It's also wise to have a range of sewing-machine bobbins loaded with different-coloured threads, ready for your projects.

GENERAL HABERDASHERY
You can lift a project out of the ordinary by choosing the details carefully. Start looking in unusual places for useful items – often, stationery and homeware shops will have good additions to your stash. Be prepared to adapt other materials to find the look you desire. For example, coloured elastic might be difficult to find but bright hair elastics can be cut and used instead. You will also need a supply of buttons in various sizes, eyelets and bias binding to finish the projects.

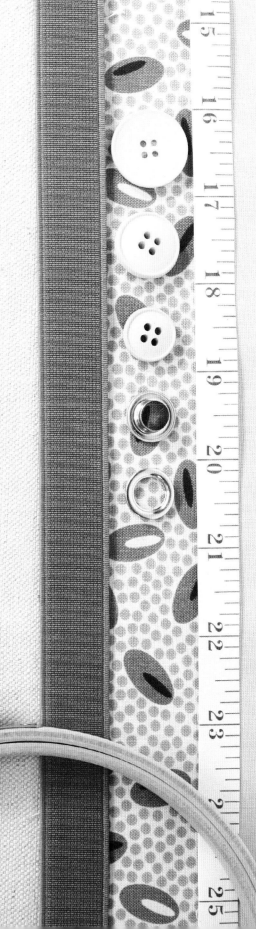

TECHNIQUES

Life's too short for complicated techniques, which is why all the projects in this book use simple ones. Most stitching in the projects is done on a sewing machine using straight or zigzag stitch. You will need to hand sew openings used for turning work.

BOX CORNER

This box corner provides a base for a bag so it stands up when packed with items. This technique is used for the Tote Bag on page 26.

1 With right sides together, pin then sew the side seams and lower seam of the bag. Press the seams open with an iron.

2 With the bag wrong sides out, press the side seam and the base seam together, working from the corner inwards. Measure 2in (5cm) along the seam from the corner, mark with a water-erasable pen, then draw a line across at right angles. Pin the fabric, then sew along the marked line.

3 Use a pair of scissors to trim off the corner.

Tip
Test out your machine stitch size and tension on a scrap of the fabric you are working with before starting the project and adjust if necessary.

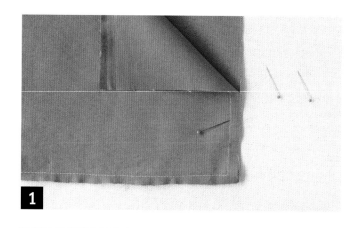

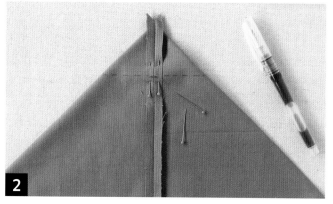

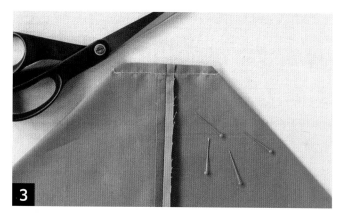

FITTING A BASE TO A CYLINDER

It can be tricky fitting a circle of fabric to a cylinder but marking the circle in quarters makes light work of it. This technique is helpful for making the Shoe-Cleaning Kit (see page 52) and the Storage Bucket (see page 100).

1 Fold the fabric for the base in quarters and mark quarter points with a water-erasable pen. Using the side seam as a quarter point, fold the cylinder in quarters and mark each quarter with the water-erasable pen. Pin the base to the cylinder, matching the marked quarter points.

2 Sew the circle and the cylinder together. Trim the seam and cut notches into it.

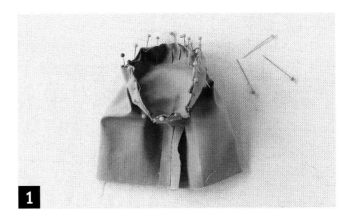

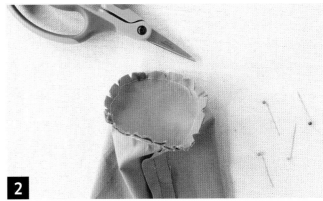

ELASTIC BUTTONHOLE

It's easy to sew a loop of elastic into a seam and it makes a great alternative to a buttonhole. This is used for the Wash Bag project on page 92.

1 Cut the elastic to length. It will need to fit snugly around the button when fastened. Bring the two cut ends together to make a loop. With the loop facing inwards, pin the cut ends in position on the right side of the fabric.

2 With right sides together, pin another piece of fabric the same size on top and sew the two pieces of fabric together to secure the buttonhole elastic. Fold the fabric right sides out and press along the seam. Avoid pressing the elastic or it could melt.

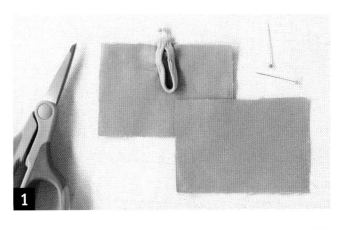

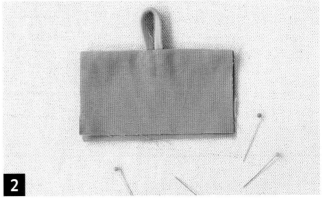

HANGING LOOP

This is a strong loop that will take the weight of large items. It works well for projects such as the Trimmed Guest Towel on page 88.

1 With right sides out, fold the strip of loop fabric in half lengthways. Press the fold to crease. Open out the fabric and fold in the outside edges to meet on the crease. Press this fold to crease.

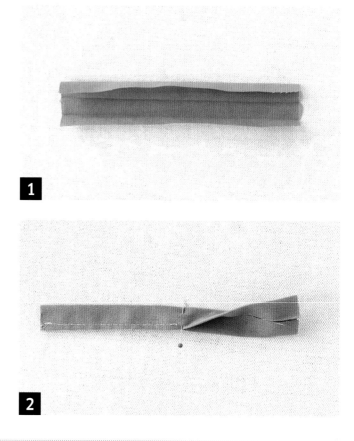

2 Fold the strip in half again so all the raw edges are hidden. Pin and machine sew along the turned edge to close.

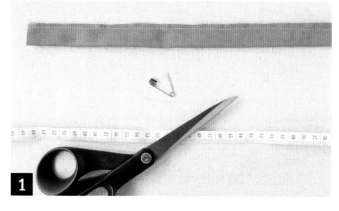

TUBULAR LOOP

An alternative way of making a loop, the tubular loop technique is used for the Pot Holder project on page 30. It is also used to make the handles for the Tote Bag on page 26.

1 With right sides together, fold the strip of fabric in half lengthways. Press the fold to crease. Sew along the length with a ¼in (6mm) seam allowance to form a tube.

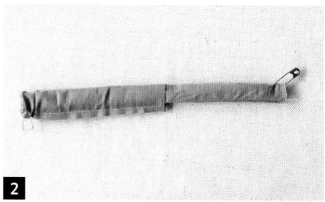

2 To turn right sides out, insert a safety pin at one end of the strip. Push the safety pin into the fabric tube then pull through and out of the opening at the opposite end. Pull the rest of the neatened loop strip through and out.

INSERTING A ZIP

Zips are easy to fit using this method. You will need to insert a zip for the Shoe Bag project on page 78.

1 Neaten the cut edge of the fabric with zigzag stitches, then turn the edge by ⅜in (1cm) and press to crease.

2 With right sides outwards, pin the zip to the edge of the fabric.

3 Use the zipper foot to sew the zip in place.

4 About 2in (5cm) before you reach the zipper slider, stop sewing. With the needle down, raise the zipper foot and pull the zipper slider 1¼in (3cm) past the raised foot. Lower the zipper foot and continue sewing to the end of the zip.

5 Repeat steps 1–4 on the other side of the zip to complete.

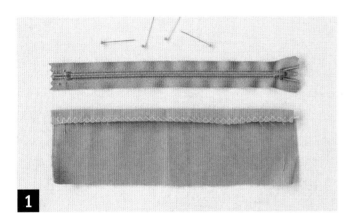

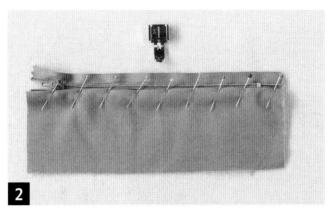

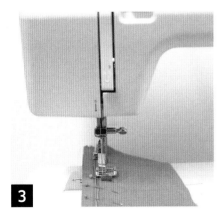

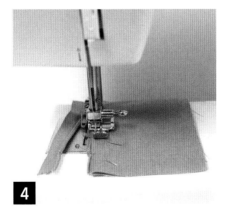

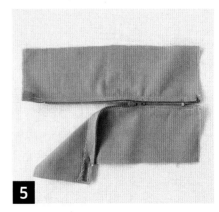

ZIP FOR A LINED BAG

This technique for zip insertion sandwiches the zip edge between the lining and outside fabric. It is used when making the Wash Bag on page 92.

1 Cut out two pieces of outside and lining fabric. With right sides together, pin the side of the zip onto the edge of one of the pieces of outside fabric. Turn over and repeat with the lining fabric, sandwiching the zip.

2 Use the zipper foot to sew through the fabrics to secure the zip.

3 Repeat steps 2–3 on the other side of the zip using the remaining pieces of outer and lining fabric (3a, 3b).

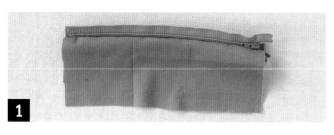

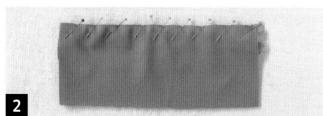

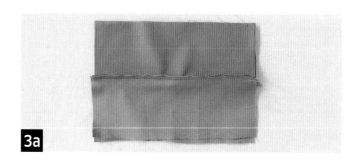

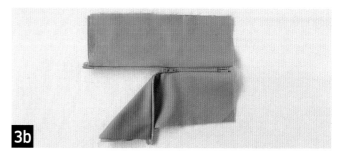

FRENCH SEAM

This is an efficient was to prevent the raw edges of a seam from fraying. The seam completely encases the raw edges, leaving a neat finish, and is ideal for items which get a lot of wear or are reversible. It is used for the Shoe Bag on page 78.

1 Trim the seam to ¼in (6mm).

2 Turn your work wrong side out. Press the seam and pin or tack along it. You will now have encased the raw edges completely within the seam.

3 Machine stitch a ⅜in (1cm) seam. Press to one side with a hot iron.

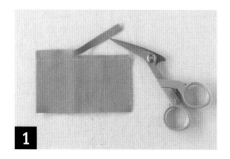

EYELETS

These add professional detail to a project. For best results, hammer on a firm surface, such as a sturdy workbench. Eyelets are used for the Lavender Bag project on page 70.

1 Put the fabric in position over the flat side of the circular piece of metal. Take the eyelet tool and place it on the fabric where you want the eyelet. Give it a firm rap with a hammer.

2 Press out the cut circle of fabric and press a collared eyelet through the hole from the reverse. Then put on the ridged side of the circular piece of metal. Place a ring eyelet on the collared eyelet to sandwich the fabric between the two eyelet sections. Place the tool on top of the eyelet ring, then tap firmly with the hammer to seal the eyelet closed.

TOP STITCHING

This gives a decorative finish and holds layers neatly in place. Top stitching is used for several projects, such as the Drinks Coaster on page 106.

1 With wrong sides facing, press the seam to one side.

2 Fold right sides out and press to crease along the seam line.

3 Stitch along the edge close to the fold, sewing as straight and as evenly as possible.

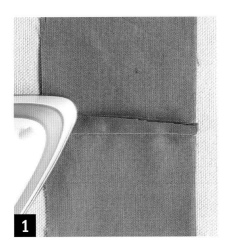

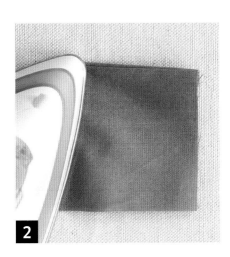

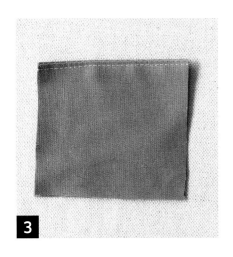

KITCHEN/
DINER

TEA COSY

To make an interesting design for this tea cosy different fabrics were used, but you can make the cosy from one piece. Alternatively, use a patterned fabric for the front and a plain fabric for the back. The lining material was also used for the edging and tab.

Find the templates on pages 130–131

You will need
1 fat quarter of main fabric
1 fat quarter of contrast fabric
2 fat quarters of lining fabric
11½ x 27in (29 x 69cm) of wadding
Tracing paper or baking parchment
Pencil
Tape measure or ruler
Pins
Scissors
Dress-making scissors
Sewing machine
Sewing needle
Thread to match fabric
Iron and ironing board

NOTE: The finished size is approximately 12½ x 10in (32 x 25cm), which is suitable for a six-cup teapot. You can easily resize the template to suit your teapot.

1 Photocopy the templates on pages 130–131 and trace over them onto tracing paper or baking parchment. Cut out with a pair of paper-cutting scissors to make the patterns. Pin the patterns onto the fabrics. Cut two outside main pieces, two bands for the bottom of the cosy, two linings and two pieces of wadding for the inside cover. Cut a 2 x 25in (5 x 64cm) strip of fabric for the edging: you can achieve the length by stitching pieces together using a ⅜in (1cm) seam and pressing open with a hot iron. Cut a 1 x 4in (2.5 x 10cm) strip for the tab.

2 Using a ⅜in (1cm) seam allowance, machine stitch the fabric band to the lower part of the pattern for both the front and the back of the cosy. Press the seam open.

3 To make the tab, fold the strip in half lengthways. Join the ends, and with the sewing machine, stitch along the length, close to the edge. Fold the tab in half.

4 Take the two outside main pieces, and with right sides together, pin around the curved and side edges, sandwiching the tab in the middle of the curve.

5 Machine stitch the two pieces of wadding together around the curved and side edges and do the same with the lining. Trim and cut notches in all the curved seams so that the seams are smooth when turned inside out.

6 Turn the outside and lining right sides out and press along the seam. Now turn the lining inside out again.

7 Layer the tea cosy by pushing the wadding into the cover, then push in the lining. Pin and tack the three layers together along the base.

8 Join the ends of the edging strip using a ⅜in (1cm) seam allowance. On the inside of the cosy, pin and tack the edging strip to the base first, then turn it over the edge, and fold the raw edge of the strip on the outside to neaten. Use the sewing machine to stitch together.

Tip

To save time, you could use a piece of ribbon or lace folded in two instead of making a tab.

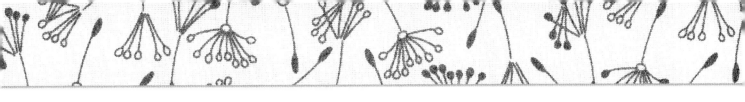

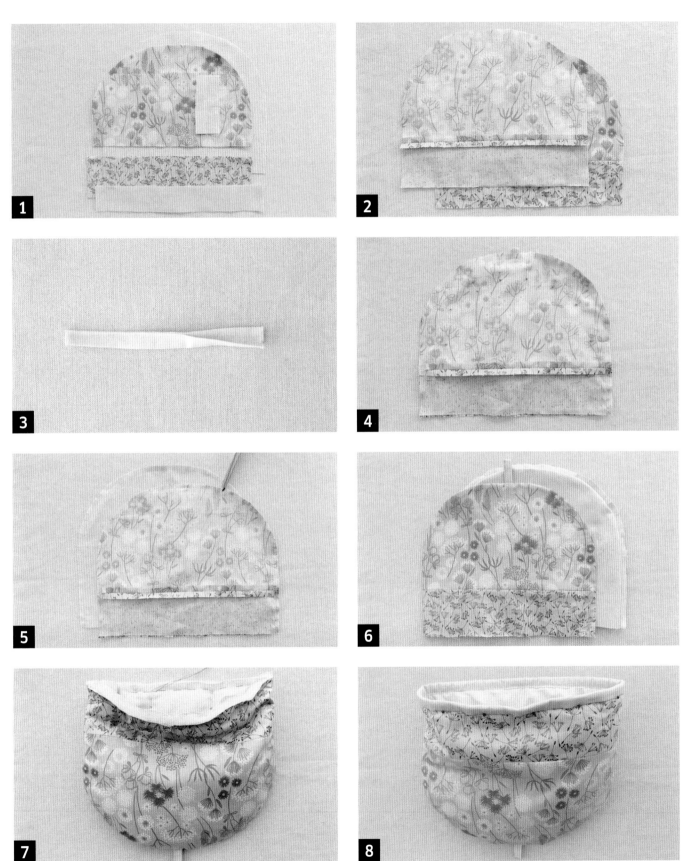

TOTE BAG

Every fabric stash should have some calico — it's inexpensive, readily available and great to use as a stabilizer when the project fabric doesn't have enough body. Calico is also perfect as a lining material, as you'll discover when you make this stylish tote bag.

You will need
2 fat quarters of main fabric
1 fat quarter of contrast fabric
2 pieces of calico, 15¾ x 15¾in (40 x 40cm), for the lining
Tape measure or ruler
Pins
Water-erasable pen
Dress-making scissors
Sewing machine
Thread to match fabric
Iron and ironing board
Safety pin
Sewing needle

NOTE: Each handle strip can be made by stitching two 2¾ x 16in (7 x 40cm) strips together using a ⅜in (1cm) seam and pressing open with a hot iron.

Tip
To save time, instead of making handles use pieces of canvas webbing — it's durable and is available in many colours.

1 From the main fabric, cut two rectangles 10¼ x 15¾in (26 x 40cm). From the contrast fabric, cut two rectangles 6¼ x 15¾in (16 x 40cm), plus two strips 2¾ x 30in (7 x 76cm) for the handles. To make the outside of the bag, pin then machine stitch one piece each of the main and contrast fabric together, using a ⅜in (1cm) seam allowance. Press the seam open. Repeat with the other pieces of main and contrast fabric.

2 With right sides facing, pin then machine stitch the side seams and bottom seam of the outer bag.

3 Pin then machine stitch the side seams and bottom seam of the calico pieces to make the lining. Leave an opening of 3¼in (8.5cm) in one of the lining side seams.

4 To make the squared base, with the bag wrong side out, press the side seam and the base seam of the outer bag together from the corner out. From the corner measure 2in (5cm) along the seam, mark with a water-erasable pen then draw a line across at right angles. Pin, then machine stitch along the marked line and trim off the corner. Repeat with the remaining corners of the outer bag and the lining. See also Box Corner technique, page 14.

5 Make the handles. With right sides together, fold one strip in half lengthways and iron to crease. Machine stitch using a ⅜in (1cm) seam allowance to form a tube. To turn right sides out, insert a safety pin at one end of the strip. Push the safety pin into the fabric tube then pull through and out of the opening at the opposite end. Pull the rest of the handle through and out, remove the safety pin, then iron. Repeat for the second handle. See also Tubular Loop, page 16.

6 To attach the handles, pin them in place at the top edge of the outer bag with a seam allowance of 1¼in (3cm). With right sides together, pin the lining to the outer fabric, matching up the side seams. Machine stitch around the top of the bags.

7 Turn the bag through the opening in the lining. Hand sew the opening closed with a needle and thread. Iron along the top edge of the bag. Sew two lines of top stitch (see page 19) ¼in (6mm) and 1¼in (3cm) along the top edge of the bag. This anchors the handles firmly in place.

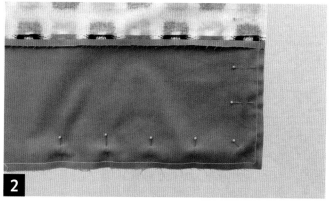

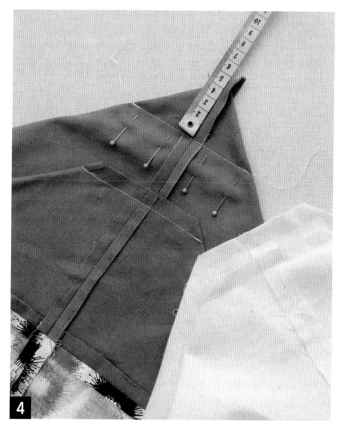

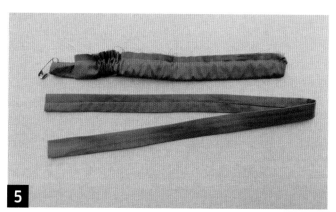

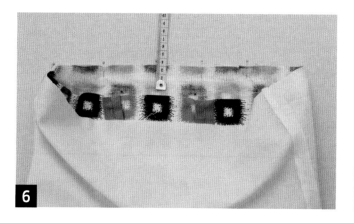

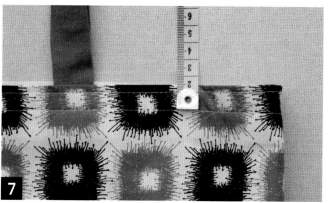

POT HOLDER

Stylish contrasting fabrics make a pot holder that will look good in any modern kitchen, but you could make the holder from one piece of fabric if you prefer. The double layer of fleece ensures you will not burn your hands when handling hot dishes.

You will need
Three contrasting fabrics:
1 fat quarter of fabric A
1 piece of fabric B, 5 x 7in (12.5 x 18cm)
1 piece of fabric C, 1¾ x 4½in (4.5 x 12cm)
2 pieces of fusible fleece, 7 x 7in (18 x 18cm)
Tape measure or ruler
Pins
Dress-making scissors
Iron and ironing board
Sewing machine
Thread to match fabric
Sewing needle
Safety pin

NOTE: You can make three pot holders from one fat quarter of fabric. This is a great project for using up fabric remnants.

1 From fabric A, cut one 7in (18cm) square for the back and two rectangles measuring 2 x 7in (5 x 18cm) for the front. Assemble all the fabric pieces. Note that a ⅜in (1cm) seam allowance has been included to use throughout.

2 To make the front of the pot holder, pin fabric B between the two rectangular pieces of fabric A. Machine stitch them together with a ⅜in (1cm) seam allowance. Press the seams open.

3 Place the adhesive side of the fusible fleece onto the wrong side of the square you have just made and onto the wrong side of the back piece (the square of fabric A). Iron to bond.

4 To make the hanging loop, with right sides together, fold fabric C in half along the length, pin, then machine stitch with a ¼in (6mm) seam allowance to form a long tube.

To turn right sides out, insert a safety pin at one end of the strip. Push the safety pin into the fabric tube then pull through and out of the opening at the opposite end. Pull the rest of the loop strip through and out. See also Tubular Loop, page 16.

5 Place the two squares right sides together. Sandwich the hanging loop in one of the corners. Pin the squares and machine stitch around all the edges with a ⅜in (1cm) seam allowance, leaving an opening of 3in (7.5cm) on one side. Clip the corners and trim the seams. Pull the pot holder through the side opening so the right sides are outwards.

6 Slip stitch the side opening closed with a needle and thread.

Tip

For a very sharp corner, use a safety pin to gently ease out the material, then press carefully.

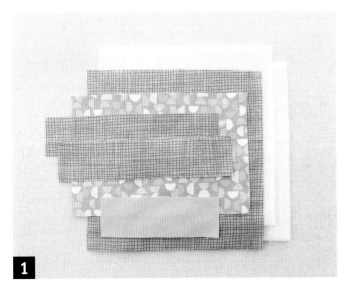

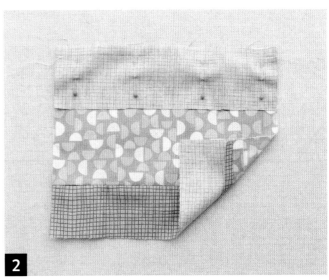

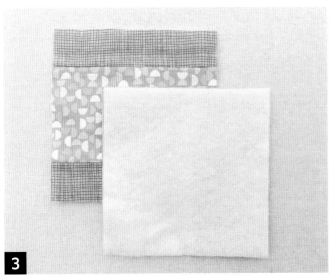

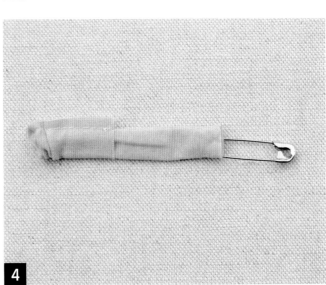

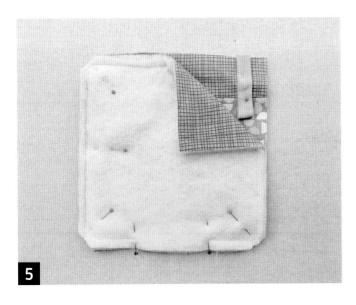

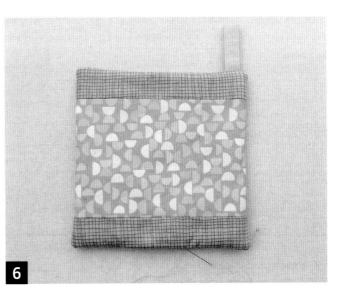

DROP-IN SEAT

Dining-room chairs are expensive items, and it is usually the seat fabric that wears out first. Instead of purchasing a new chair, why not freshen it up by simply re-covering the seat? Choose fabric that complements the style of your chair to maximize the look.

You will need
Screwdriver
Fabric to fit the seat plus enough for a 4in (10cm) overlap
    all the way around (2 continuous fat quarters for a seat with
    a maximum seat measurement of 14in (35cm)
Calico to fit the base of the seat plus enough for a ⅜in (1cm)
    overlap all the way round
Tape measure or ruler
Staple gun
Dress-making scissors
Pins
Iron and ironing board

1 Using the screwdriver, unscrew the seat from the frame.

2 Place the seat face down on the fabric. Fold the fabric over the edge of the seat and cut it out, making sure you leave a 4in (10cm) overlap.

3 With the seat face down on the wrong side of the fabric, staple the fabric onto the back of the seat, working from the middle of the seat edge towards the corners.

4 When you reach a corner, fold the fabric over the corner of the seat and staple in the middle.

5 Fold and turn the edge fabric on one side over the corner and staple it down.

6 Repeat on the other side of the corner. Continue to staple the fabric along the edges of the seat and repeat steps 4–6 when you reach the other corners.

7 Fold over the edges of the calico ⅜in (1cm) all the way round. Press, then staple in place underneath the seat so that the edges of the new cover are now concealed. Screw the seat back onto the base.

Tip

If your chair seat is wider than 18in (46cm), sew strips of a coordinating fabric to the sides of the main fabric so they tuck under the chair.

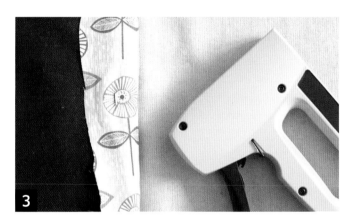

CAFETIÈRE COVER

This simple cafetière cover uses very little fabric and is reversible, so you get two very different looks for the price of one. It makes the perfect present for those difficult-to-buy-for friends who have everything except for a designer cafetière cover.

Find the template on page 131

You will need
1 fat quarter of main fabric
1 fat quarter of contrast fabric
7 x 14in (18 x 35.5cm) of lining fabric
7 x 14in (18 x 35.5cm) of fusible fleece
1 piece of hook-and-loop tape, 1 x 2in (2.5 x 5cm)
Tape measure or ruler
Tracing paper or baking parchment
Pencil
Scissors
Pins
Dress-making scissors
Sewing machine
Thread to match fabric
Sewing needle
Iron and ironing board

NOTE: You can make the cover from one fat quarter if you use the same material for the whole project.

1 From the main fabric, cut one 4 x 14in (10 x 35.5cm) rectangle. From the contrast fabric, cut two pieces measuring 2½ x 14in (6.5 x 35.5cm). To construct the different sections of the outer fabric, arrange the main piece of fabric to form the central part, and the two contrast pieces of fabric for the top and bottom strips.

2 Using a ⅜in (1cm) seam allowance, pin and then machine sew one long side of the top piece of contrast fabric to one of the long sides of the main fabric Repeat on the other side of the main fabric with the other piece of contrast fabric. Trim the seams and press open.

3 Photocopy the template on page 131 and trace over it onto tracing paper or baking parchment. Cut out with a pair of paper-cutting scissors to make a pattern. Pin the pattern to your constructed piece of outer fabric and cut out. Repeat with the lining fabric and fusible fleece.

4 Place the adhesive side of the fusible fleece on the wrong side of the lining and iron to bond.

5 With right sides together, pin the lining to the constructed piece of outer fabric. Machine stitch around the edge with a ⅜in (1cm) seam allowance, leaving an opening of 4in (10cm) on the lower edge for turning. Trim the seam and clip the corners.

6 Turn the cafetière cover through the seam opening. Fold in the opening seam allowance, iron, then slip stitch the opening closed with a needle and thread.

7 Measure the length of the tabs and cut a piece of hook-and-loop tape to fit. Stitch in place with the sewing machine.

Tip

Baking parchment is great for patterns – it's easy to get hold of, inexpensive and translucent, which makes quick work of tracing.

HOW TO MAKE A BESPOKE COVER

This cover is designed to fit a standard eight-cup vessel with a circumference of 12in (30.5cm). To make a pattern for another size of cafetière, measure the circumference and height of the beaker from just under the pouring spout to the bottom of the glass. Draw these measurements on paper and round off the four corners. Add tabs for fastening, about 1in (2.5cm) wide by 2in (5cm) long. The tabs should be positioned halfway down the centre of each opening. Add a ⅜in (1cm) seam allowance all around the pattern. Cut out and use as a template.

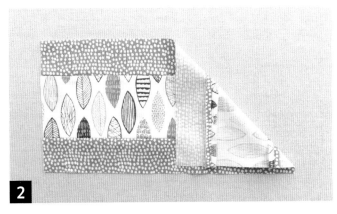

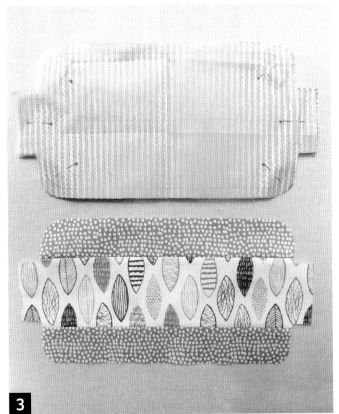

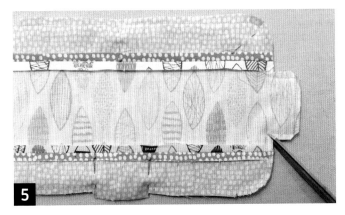

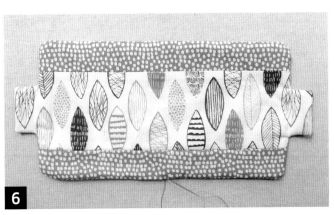

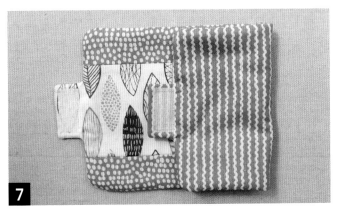

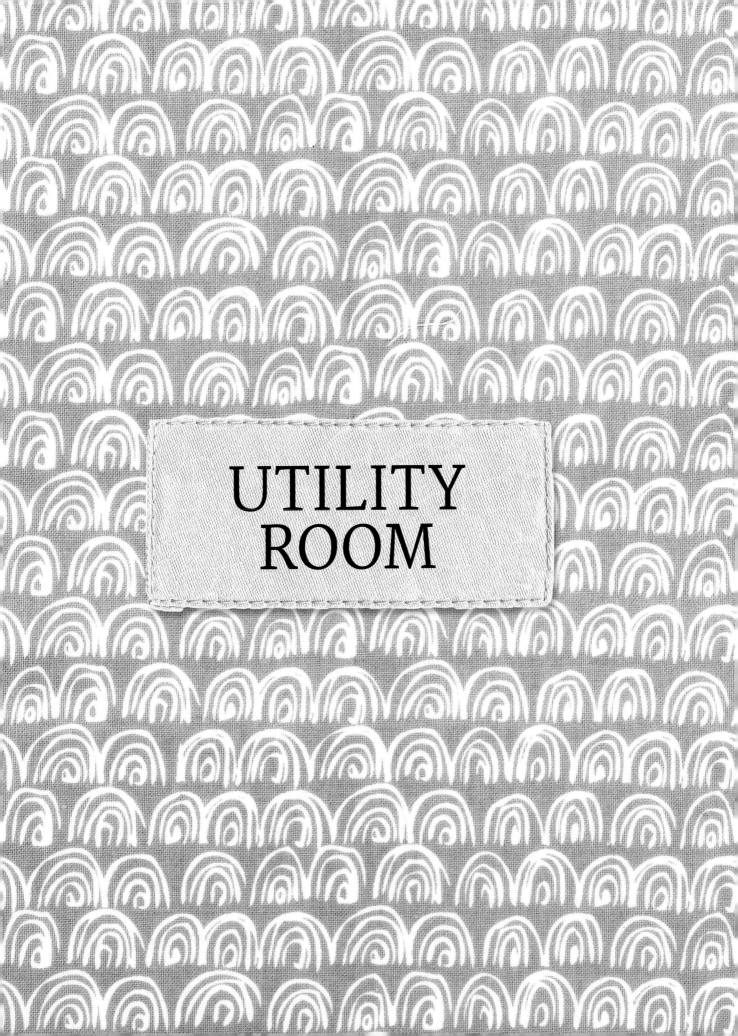

UTILITY ROOM

PEG BAG

It's great to have pegs close at hand when you're wrestling wet washing onto the line. This bucket-style bag is simply perfect for the job — it hangs on the line so it's easy to dip into it and grab the pegs as you need them. Just bring it inside when it rains!

Find the templates on page 132

You will need
1 fat quarter of main fabric
1 fat quarter of lining fabric
$13^{1}/_{2}$ x 16in (34 x 41cm) of fusible interfacing
Tape measure or ruler
Tracing paper or baking parchment
Pencil
Scissors
Pins
Sewing machine
Thread to match fabric
Sewing needle
Dress-making scissors
Iron and ironing board
Hook

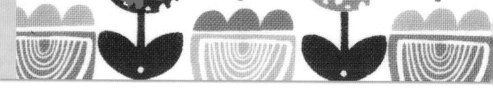

1 Photocopy the templates on page 132 and trace over them onto tracing paper or baking parchment. Cut out with a pair of paper-cutting scissors to make the patterns. Pin the patterns to the main fabric, lining fabric and fusible interfacing, and cut out one of each. Iron the fusible interfacing onto the wrong side of the base and side pieces of the main fabric.

2 To make the peg bag sides, with right sides facing, pin together the main and lining fabrics. Using a ⅜in (1cm) seam allowance throughout, machine stitch along the top seam. Trim and cut notches along the seam.

3 Open out the fabric. With right sides facing, pin and machine stitch the side seam of the lining and the main fabric to form a tube. Leave a gap of 3¼in (8cm) in the lining seam for turning.

4 Clip into the seam above and below the point where the main fabric and lining meet. To make fitting the base to the sides easier, mark the quarter points on the open ends of the tube and the bases. With right sides facing, pin the base to the main fabric, matching the quarter points, then repeat with the lining. Machine stitch in position, then trim the seams and cut notches along them close to the stitching. See also Fitting a Base to a Cylinder, page 15.

5 Turn the bag through the opening in the side seam. Iron the seams flat, turn in the edge of the opening, then slip stitch the opening closed with a needle and thread.

6 Turn the top point under by ½in (1.2cm) then fold in by 1in (2.5cm). Iron flat, and machine stitch along the edge to form a loop. Push the hook through the loop.

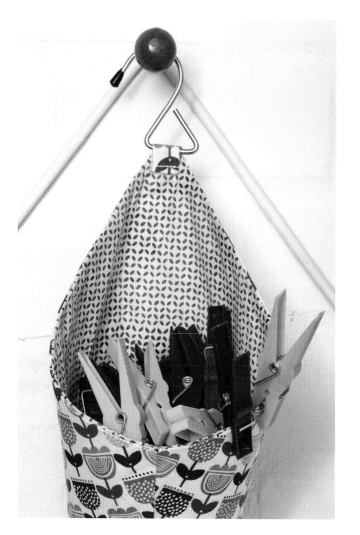

Tip

If you can't find a hook like the one pictured, use a butcher's hook instead.

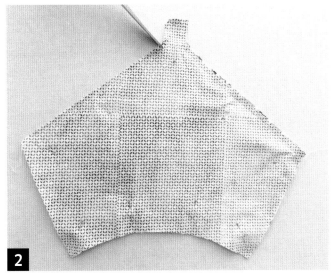

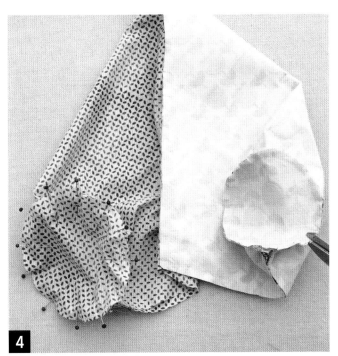

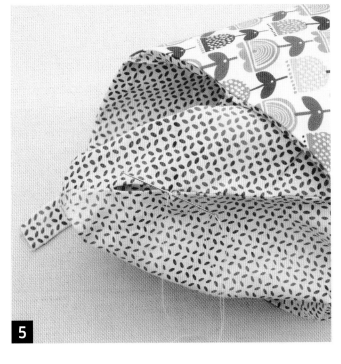

HALF APRON

An apron is a necessity in the kitchen but there's no reason why it shouldn't be stylish, too. This is a quick and easy project which updates a retro design with modern fabrics, and comes with a handy pocket for stashing essentials such as recipe cards or utensils.

You will need
1 fat quarter of main fabric
1 fat quarter of contrast fabric
19 x 30in (48 x 76cm) of calico for the lining
60in (180cm) length of 1¼in (3cm)-wide webbing for the ties
Tape measure or ruler
Pins
Dress-making scissors
Iron and ironing board
Sewing machine
Thread to match fabric

1 From the main fabric and calico, cut a 15 x 22in (38 x 56cm) rectangle. With right sides out, put the main fabric and calico lining together. Turn the short sides of the apron in by ⅜in (1cm), iron, then turn in again by the same amount and iron. Now do the same with the long sides. Open out the folds and cut off the corners.

2 To make the ties, cut the length of webbing in half and place each piece near the top of the short sides of the apron. Refold and pin around all the hems to secure them, making sure the ends of the webbing are tucked under the hem. With a sewing machine, stitch all around the edges of the apron, using a ⅜in (1cm) seam allowance throughout.

3 Fold the ties out and add an extra line of machine stitching at the side to keep them in place. Neaten the raw ends by turning in by ⅜in (1cm), then turn in again by the same amount and machine stitch down.

4 To make the pocket strip, cut a 7½ x 13½in (19 x 34cm) rectangle from the contrast fabric and the calico lining. With right sides together, using a ⅜in (1cm) seam allowance, pin and machine sew the pocket around the edge, leaving one of the long sides open. Trim the seams and cut off the corners.

5 Turn the pocket right sides out. Press flat, then turn the top edge over by ⅜in (1cm) and iron. Turn again by the same amount, iron once more, then machine stitch down.

6 To position the pocket on the apron, fold the apron and pocket in half widthways and make a crease. Position the pocket centrally. Pin, then machine stitch around three edges of the pocket, leaving the top open.

Tip

You can make the apron in calico instead of printed fabric and then personalize it with your own design using fabric felt-tip pens.

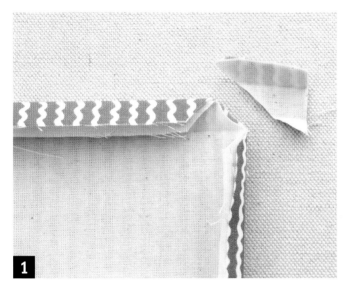

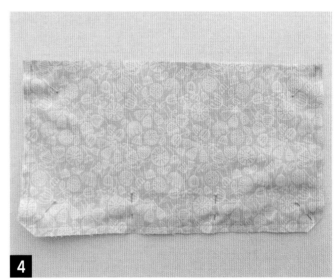

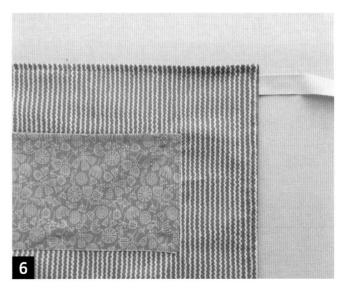

SHOE-CLEANING KIT

Looking for all the bits and bobs needed for shoe cleaning can make the whole process even more of a hassle. Round up all the items and store them in this bag with its handy side pockets. Just add elbow grease for a perfect shine!

Find the templates on page 133

You will need
2 fat quarters of main fabric
2 fat quarters of contrast fabric
18 x 30in (46 x 76cm) of fusible interfacing
Tape measure or ruler
Tracing paper or baking parchment
Pencil
Scissors
Pins
Dress-making scissors
Water-erasable pen
Sewing machine
Thread to match fabric
Iron and ironing board
Sewing needle

NOTE: You could sew oddments together with ⅜in (1cm) seams, pressed open, to create pieces big enough for the patterns.

1 Photocopy the templates on page 133 and trace over them onto tracing paper or baking parchment. Cut out with a pair of paper-cutting scissors to make the patterns. Pin the patterns to the fabrics and fusible interfacing and cut out. To transfer the pattern markings onto the pocket strip and main fabric, make a hole with the point of scissors through the pattern piece, then using a water-erasable pen mark with a dot, square or a triangle, as appropriate.

2 Iron the fusible interfacing onto the wrong side of the fabrics to stiffen them. The fusible interfacing for the base should be ironed onto the wrong side of the main fabric base piece. Note that the rectangles of interfacing are slightly smaller than the main and contrast fabric (⅜in/1cm) so that the seam allowance is not too bulky at each side and along the bottom.

3 To make the pocket strip, with right sides out fold the main fabric in half lengthways and machine stitch closed along the base using a ⅜in (1cm) seam allowance. Mark the position of the channels with pins on both the pocket fabric and on the fabric for the inner bag.

4 Pin both ends of the pocket strip to the bottom of the short edges of the inner bag fabric. Machine stitch with a ⅜in (1cm) seam allowance. Pin down the pocket channels and stitch in place.

5 To make the pleats in the pockets, pin a few millimetres either side of the sewn channel and then press. For the two end pockets, leave a gap before the pleats of ⅜in (1cm) for the seam allowance. Pin and machine stitch along the lower edge of the pleats to secure them.

6 Turn the bag wrong sides out and machine stitch up the side seam with a ⅜in (1cm) seam allowance, leaving a gap of 4in (10cm) in the inside seam of the main bag for turning.

7 To make it easier to position the base, mark the quarter points on the open ends of the bag and the bases. Matching the quarter points, pin the circular bases in place at the bottom of the lining and the outer bag, and machine stitch with a ⅜in (1cm) seam allowance. Trim the seams and cut notches. See also Fitting a Base to a Cylinder, page 15.

8 Turn the bag right sides out through the side seam opening and sew closed with a needle and thread.

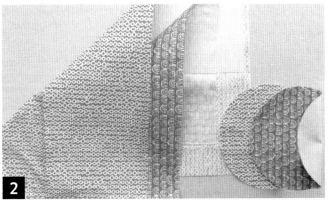

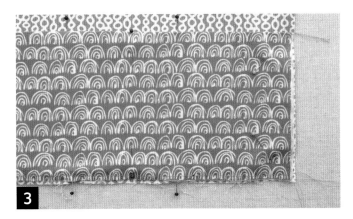

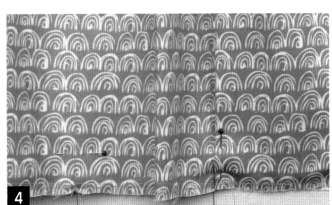

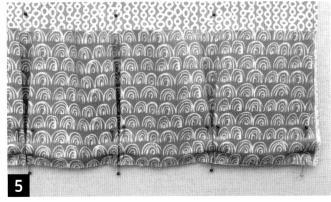

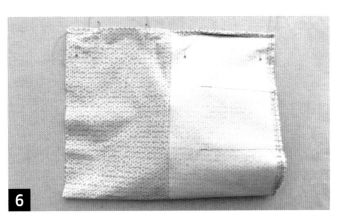

PLASTIC-BAG TIDY

No one should be throwing away plastic bags these days. This is a really attractive and practical way to keep your old plastic carrier bags readily available for reuse. It keeps the bags orderly and out of sight but it is easy to grab one when needed.

You will need
1 fat quarter of main fabric
1 fat quarter of contrast fabric
36in (91cm) length of ½in (12mm)-wide elastic
Tape measure or ruler
Sewing needle
Pins
Dress-making scissors
Sewing machine
Thread to match fabric
Iron and ironing board
Safety pin

1 From the main piece of fabric cut one piece 14 x 18in (36 x 46cm) to form the body of the holder. For the casing, cut two pieces of contrast fabric 6 x 18in (15 x 46cm). For the loop, cut one piece of contrast fabric 2 x 6in (5 x 15cm).

2 To neaten the casing, turn in the short sides of the contrast fabric by ⅜in (1cm). Press flat and machine sew with a straight stitch. Repeat with the other piece of contrast fabric.

3 With wrong sides facing, take the loop piece and fold it in half lengthways. Press flat. Open up and fold each raw edge to the crease just made with the iron. Fold in half again so all the raw edges are hidden. Machine sew with a straight stitch close to the edge.

4 With right sides together, pin the contrast fabric ⅜in (1cm) in from the long edge of the main fabric. Using a ⅜in (1cm) seam allowance, machine stitch the contrast strip to the main fabric. Repeat this step along the bottom edge of the main fabric with the other piece of contrast fabric.

5 Fold over the long raw casing edge by ¼in (6mm) and press flat, to neaten. Turn the top edge over by 3in (7.5cm) onto the main body fabric, to create a casing. Pin and machine sew two lines of stitching, one close to the top edge and one 1in (2.5cm) below, making a channel for the elastic. Repeat this step with the other piece of contrast fabric, at the bottom edge of the main fabric, so that there will be a casing at the top and bottom of the bag.

6 Fold and pin the bag in half lengthways, so the wrong side is facing outwards. Pin the hanging loop just below one side of the casing, so it is facing inwards. Making sure to leave the casings open at either side, using a ⅜in (1cm) seam allowance, machine stitch down the side seam to create a tube. Turn the right way out.

7 Cut the elastic in half. Pin the safety pin onto one end of the elastic and thread the elastic through one of the casings. Knot the ends of the elastic so that it forms a circle. It should be slack enough so that you can grab a bag but tight enough that the bags won't fall out. Push the knot into the casing so that it is hidden. Thread the remaining piece of elastic through the other casing and repeat this step so that there is an elasticated end at the top and bottom of the bag.

Tip
Make this bag in different sizes for storing other items, such as cotton wool or tennis balls.

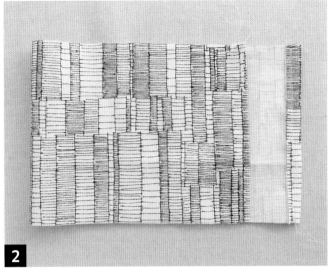

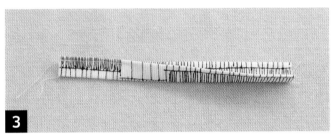

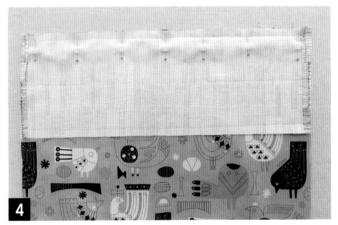

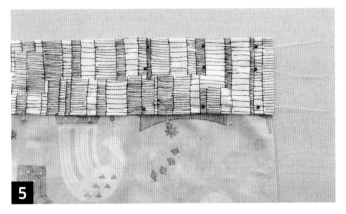

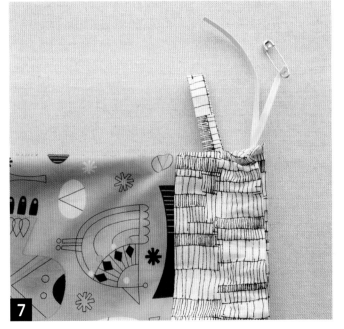

LINGERIE WASH BAG

It's always handy to have a small bag to keep your delicate lingerie separate from the rest of your laundry, particularly if they are made from expensive fabrics. You could also use this attractive bag for storing other small items when you go on holiday.

You will need
1 fat quarter of main fabric
1 fat quarter of contrast fabric
20in (50cm) length of ½in (12mm)-wide elastic
Pins
Tape measure or ruler
Dress-making scissors
Sewing machine
Thread to match fabric
Iron and ironing board
Large safety pin

1 From the main fabric, cut one piece 13½ x 21in (34 x 53cm). From the contrast fabric, cut two pieces 13½ x 9½in (34 x 24cm), and a strip 2 x 6in (5 x 15cm) for the loop. With right sides facing, using a ⅜in (1cm) seam allowance, pin and machine sew one long side of each piece of contrast fabric to the 13½in (34cm) side of either end of the main body fabric. Fold in the edges of the contrast fabric by ⅜in (1cm). Press flat.

2 Make the loop. With wrong sides facing, fold the loop piece in half lengthways. Press flat. Open up and fold each raw edge to the middle crease just made with the iron. Fold in half again so all the raw edges are hidden. Pin and machine sew close to the edge with a straight stitch.

3 With right sides facing, fold the bag fabric in half lengthways and pin along the two sides. Sandwich the loop 5in (12.5cm) from the top edge, facing inwards (see middle right of photograph). Using a ⅜in (1cm) seam allowance, stitch down both sides but leave a 1½in (4cm) gap 7½in (19cm) from the top on the same side as the loop and continue the seam to the top edge.

4 Turn over the top edge to make a 4½in (12cm) hem. Pin and machine sew two lines of stitching, one close to the hem and one near the fold. Sew a third line 2in (5cm) above the lower line of stitching to make a casing.

5 Turn the bag the right way out. Fasten the safety pin to one end of the elastic and use it to push the elastic through the casing – the channel between the top two lines of stitching in Step 4. Adjust the elastic so that it is the right tension for putting items into the bag. Tie off the ends and push them into the casing so the knot is hidden.

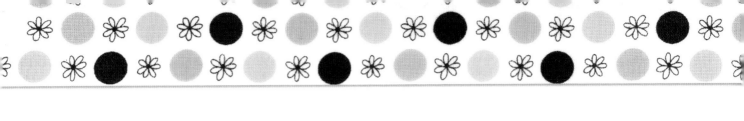

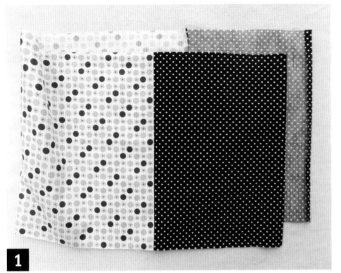

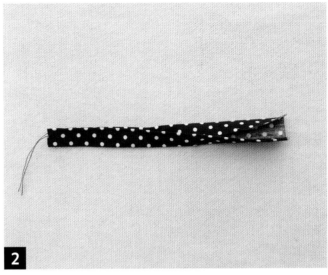

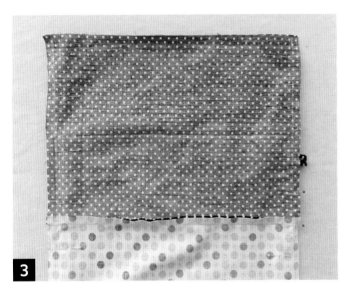

Tip

Use this bag to store tights in so that they are easy to find.

BEDROOM

DECORATED BED LINEN

This is a simple, cost-effective way to add chic detail to a plain duvet cover and pillowcase to create an attractive bed-linen set. You could even decorate the back of the cover with different contrasting fabrics to make a reversible set.

You will need
Plain duvet cover and pillowcase
2 fat quarters of main fabric to make 2 pieces measuring
    6 x 60in (15 x 152cm)
1 fat quarter of contrast fabric to make 2 pieces measuring
    3 x 60in (7.5 x 152cm)
Tape measure or ruler
Iron and ironing board
Pins
Sewing machine
Thread to match main fabric
Dress-making scissors

NOTE: You will need to piece 6in (15cm)-wide strips of main fabric and 3in (7.5cm)-wide strips of contrast fabric together to achieve the lengths specified.

1 Lay out the two pieces of main fabric and two pieces of contrast fabrics, right side up.

2 Fold both pieces of contrast fabric in half lengthways and iron to crease. Take a piece of main fabric, then pin a creased contrast strip along the top edge, right sides together. Machine stitch with a ⅜in (1cm) seam allowance. Repeat with the remaining pieces of main and contrast fabric so that you now have two made-up strips of fabric.

3 Cut one of these made-up strips into sections, one 20¾in (52.5cm) long and two 9in (23cm) long (a). The 20¾in (52.5cm)-long piece will be used to decorate the pillowcase (see step 5) and you will have another piece of made-up strip approximately 21in (53.5cm) long left over, which you could use for another pillowcase or project. Using a ⅜in (1cm) seam allowance, pin the two shorter 9in (23cm) lengths to either end of the remaining made-up strip of fabric and machine stitch together. This will make a piece wide enough for the front of a double duvet cover with a ⅜in (1cm) seam allowance at either side. Press the seams open (b).

4 Turn the top edge of the long strip along the central crease and iron it down. Turn in the remaining long and short sides by ⅜in (1cm) and then iron.

5 With the contrast strip facing down, pin the long duvet strip 7in (18cm) from the top edge of the duvet. Pin through the top, bottom and sides of the main fabric, then machine stitch in place, leaving the edging strip loose. Repeat with the pillowcase strip (the 20¾in (52.5cm)-long piece from step 3), placing it 2¾in (7cm) from the opening edge of the pillowcase.

Tip

You could use two thinner strips of fabric on your duvet cover for a different look.

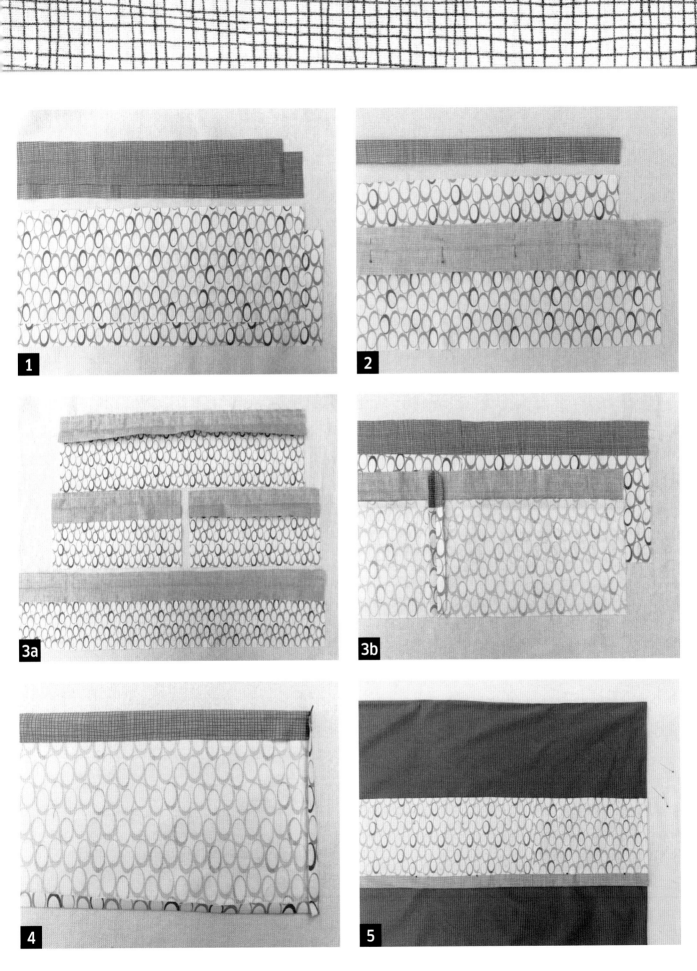

LAVENDER BAG

As well as using up scraps of fabric, this project makes good use of lavender from the garden after it has flowered. Hang your lavender bag from a coat hanger or put in a clothes drawer to add a delicate scent to your clothes. Lavender also repels moths!

You will need
1 fat quarter of fabric
6 x 13in (15 x 33cm) of fusible webbing
Tape measure or ruler
Tracing paper or baking parchment
Pencil
Scissors
Pins
Dress-making scissors
Sewing machine
Thread to match fabric
Iron and ironing board
Dry lavender
Sewing needle
¾in (2cm) eyelet and eyelet tool (or make a fabric
    hanging loop: see page 16)
Hammer

NOTE: One fat quarter will make four lavender bags.

1 Make a triangular pattern on tracing paper or baking parchment by drawing a rectangle 6 x 5¼in (15 x 13cm). Cut it out with a pair of paper-cutting scissors, then fold it in half lengthways. Mark a point ⅜in (1cm) from one corner on the open long edge. At the opposite end, on the short edge, mark a point ⅜in (1cm) from the fold. Draw a diagonal line between these two marks, then cut along the line. Open out the pattern.

2 Fold the fabric in half, pin the pattern onto it and cut out two triangles. Cut out two triangles of fusible webbing the same size and iron onto the wrong side of each fabric piece.

3 With right sides facing, pin the back piece to the front piece. Leaving a gap of 2½in (6cm), along the short edge, machine stitch round the triangle, using a ⅜in (1cm) seam allowance.

4 Trim the points of the triangle and turn the bag through so the right side faces outwards. Gently tease out the points with a pin, fold in the edges of the opening, then press flat.

5 Fill the bag with lavender using a paper cone. Do not overfill because the lavender should be able to move around. Slip stitch the side opening closed with a needle and thread.

6 Sew a top stitch (see page 19) close to the edge all the way round the bag, pushing the lavender out of the way as you go.

7 Shake the lavender to the base. Following the manufacturer's instructions, punch a hole using the eyelet tool and add an eyelet to the corner. Press the eyelet in place with the hammer. See also Eyelets, page 19.

Tip

To get a sharp point on a triangular corner, stop one stitch before the turn and do a single stitch across before turning down the next side.

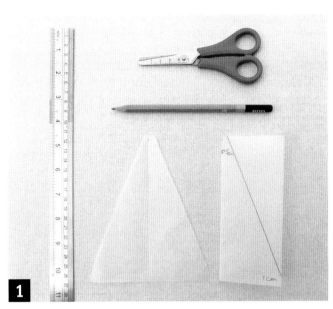

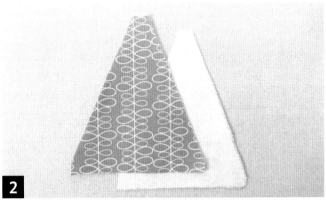

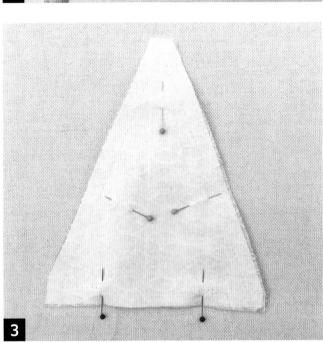

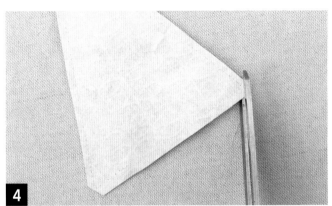

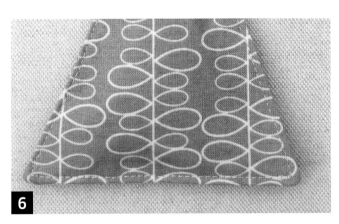

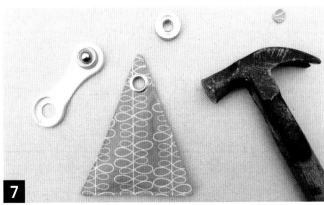

PADDED COAT HANGER

Padded coat hangers use very little fabric, and make a stylish addition to any wardrobe. They help to maintain the shape of your clothes, and the buttons near the edge are very useful for holding the loops of your skirt or trouser waistbands in place.

Find the template on page 141

You will need
1 fat quarter of fabric
1½ x 33in (4 x 84cm) of wadding
16in (40.5cm)-wide coat hanger
2 buttons in contrasting colour
Tracing paper or baking parchment
Tape measure or ruler
Pencil
Scissors
Pins
Dress-making scissors
Sewing needle
Thread to match fabric
Sewing machine
Iron and ironing board

NOTE: One fat quarter will make three coat hangers.

1 Photocopy the template on page 141 and trace over it onto tracing paper or baking parchment. Cut out with a pair of paper-cutting scissors to make a pattern. Pin the pattern onto the folded fabric and cut out.

2 Lay the coat hanger on top of the wadding so the ends meet in the middle.

3 Hand sew loosely over the wadding to hold it in place on the hanger.

4 With right sides facing, fold the fabric in half lengthways and press.

5 With a ⅜in (1cm) seam allowance, pin and machine sew the short curved side seams together. Clip the curves.

6 Turn the fabric cover the right way out, fold in the raw edges by ⅜in (1cm) and press. Place the coat hanger inside the fabric cover.

7 Pin the top edges together and hand sew the opening closed with a needle and thread.

8 Hand sew the buttons on top of the covered coat hanger 1in (2.5cm) in from either end.

Tip

You could sew this project by hand instead of using a sewing machine.

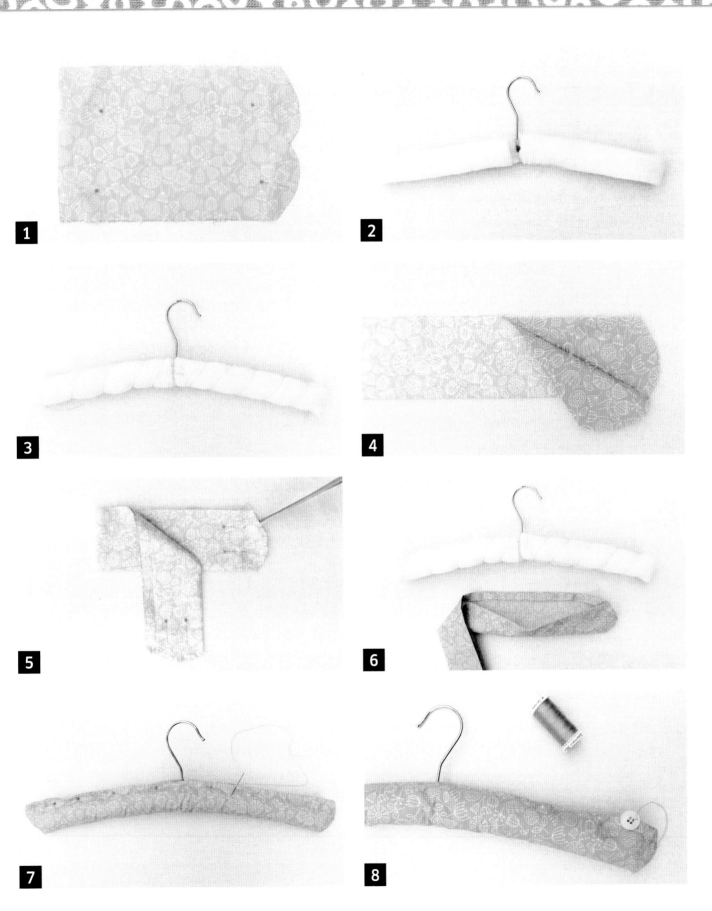

SHOE BAG

Use this handy little lightweight bag to pack your trainers in ready for the gym and keep them separate from the rest of your workout gear. It's also useful for taking shoes on holiday. French seams (see page 18) are used at the ends to give a neat finish.

You will need
1 fat quarter of main fabric
1 fat quarter of contrast fabric
16in (40cm) zip
Tape measure or ruler
Pins
Dress-making scissors
Iron and ironing board
Sewing machine
Thread to match fabric
Sewing needle
Water-erasable marker pen

1 From the main fabric cut a piece measuring 7 x 22in (18 x 56cm) and a 2 x 12in (5 x 30cm) strip for the loop. From the contrast fabric cut two pieces measuring 6½ x 22in (16.5 x 56cm) for the side panels. With a sewing machine, use zigzag stitch to neaten one long edge on each strip of fabric.

2 Make the main section of the bag. With right sides together, pin and machine sew the zigzag-neatened sides of the contrast fabric pieces to the long sides of the main fabric. Press the seams open.

3 Fold down the two shorter sides by ⅜in (1cm) and press to crease. Use zigzag stitch to neaten both edges.

4 With right sides together, place the zip on the folded short edge of the fabric. Pin then machine sew it in place, stitching as close to the teeth of the zip as possible. Repeat on the opposite edge of the fabric with the other side of the zip. See also Inserting a Zip, page 17.

5 To make the loops, use the 2 x 12in (5 x 30cm) strip of fabric. With right sides facing, fold along the length and machine stitch together with a ⅜in (1cm) seam allowance. Turn right sides out and press. Cut the strip into two lengths, 9½in (24cm) and 2½in (6cm).

Tip

This bag is made to fit a large pair of women's shoes. You could make it smaller for a child, or enlarge it for men's shoes.

6 To make pleats along the long sides, close the zip along the centre of the bag. Fold the bag into eighths and mark the position of each fold with a water-erasable marker pen. Press the long sides towards the centre, matching the markings to form pleats, and pin in position.

7 Fold both loop strips in half. With the zip closed, place the longer loop at the zip-pull end and the smaller one at the other end. Pin and sew along the bag edge to close. Repeat at the other end and trim the seams.

8 Turn the bag wrong sides out. Sew the trimmed seam with a ⅜in (1cm) seam allowance to neaten. Repeat on the seam at the other end, and turn right sides out.

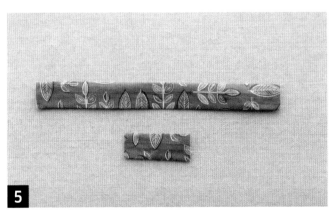

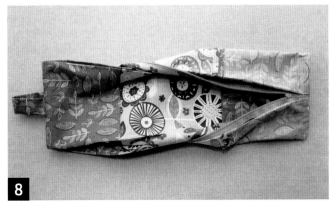

HOT-WATER BOTTLE COVER

When it is cold and miserable or you are feeling unwell, there is nothing quite as good as snuggling up with a hot-water bottle and letting the happy childhood memories flood back. A padded cover makes it particularly comforting.

Find the templates on
pages 134–135

You will need
1 fat quarter of main fabric
1 fat quarter of contrast fabric
18 x 18in (46 x 46cm) of calico
18 x 18in (46 x 46cm) of wadding
24in (61cm) length of contrast bias binding
Tape measure or ruler
Tracing paper or baking parchment
Pencil
Scissors
Pins
Dress-making scissors
Sewing machine
Thread to match fabric
Sewing needle
Iron and ironing board

1 Photocopy the templates on pages 134–135 and trace over them onto tracing paper or baking parchment. Cut out with a pair of paper-cutting scissors to make patterns. Pin the patterns for the front and lower back onto the main fabric and cut out one of each. To make the lining pieces, repeat the process on the calico and wadding. Pin the upper-back pattern onto the contrast fabric, cut out and then repeat the process on the calico and wadding to make the lining pieces.

2 With right sides facing out, sandwich the wadding between the front cover fabric and the calico lining pieces. With a ³⁄₈in (1cm) seam allowance, pin and then machine sew round the edge with a straight stitch.

3 Repeat step two with both the lower and upper-back patterns.

4 Pin the bias binding onto the back pieces of the bottle cover along the straight edges and then machine sew in place with a ³⁄₈in (1cm) seam allowance. Fold the bias over the raw edges and hand sew using a slip stitch.

5 Make a hanging loop. Cut a 4¹⁄₂in (12cm) piece of bias binding, fold it in half lengthways, covering the raw edges, and sew down its length, close to the edge. Pin the loop facing inwards and machine sew onto the top of the cover front.

6 With right sides facing and using a ³⁄₈in (1cm) seam allowance, pin then machine sew the lower back to the front cover. Then pin and machine sew the upper back to the front cover. Trim the seams.

7 Turn the cover through the right way. Note that there will be an overlap at the back of the hot-water bottle cover.

Tip

To make the hot-water bottle cover even more cosy, use thicker wadding or make it with a fleecy fabric.

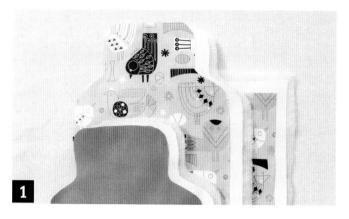

1

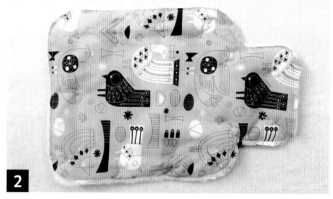

2

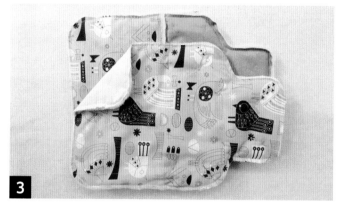

3

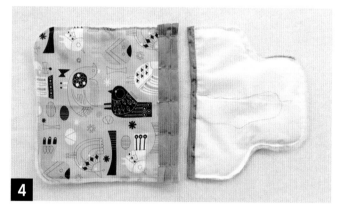

4

5

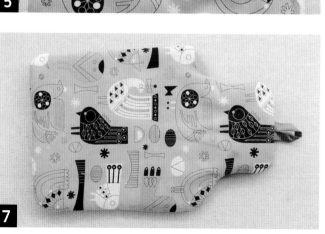

7

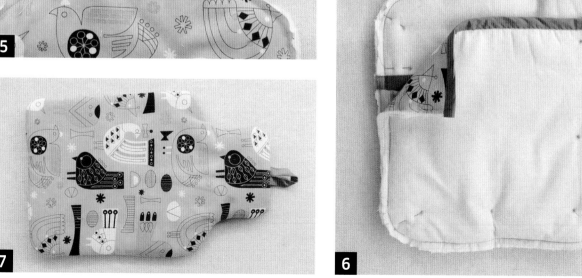

6

BATHROOM

TRIMMED GUEST TOWEL

If you like to keep a set of special towels solely for guests, why not customize them with coordinating fabric trims? This technique works best on a small hand towel but if you have more of the same fabric decorate a bath towel to match.

You will need

1 fat quarter of main fabric, or 2 pieces of prewashed fabric strips: each strip should measure the width of the towel plus a 1in (2.5cm) seam allowance x 3½in (9cm) deep

1 piece of fabric for the loop, 6 x 2in (15 x 5cm)

Tape measure or ruler

Coloured towel

Sewing machine

Thread to match fabric

Dress-making scissors

Pins

Iron and ironing board

NOTE: Quantities for this project depend on the width of your towel, but remember that you can piece scraps together with ⅜in (1cm) seams, pressed open, to create strips of fabric to the measurements required.

1 Cut the fabric into two strips, one for each end of the towel.

2 Press the strip under by ⅜in (1cm) on all sides. Repeat for the other strip.

3 If the towel has a woven border, pin the strip to cover it, making sure it is straight and all the raw edges are tucked under. If it has no woven border, pin the strip approximately 3¼in (8.5cm) from the end of the towel. With a sewing machine, stitch the strip onto the towel with a straight stitch as close to the edge as possible (approximately ⅛in/3mm).

4 Make the loop. With wrong sides facing, take the loop piece and fold it in half lengthways. Press flat. Open up and fold each raw edge to the crease you have just made with the iron. Fold in half again so all the raw edges are hidden. Machine sew close to the edge with a straight stitch. See also Hanging Loop, page 16.

5 Pin the loop at one corner of the towel, then machine sew it on using straight stitch.

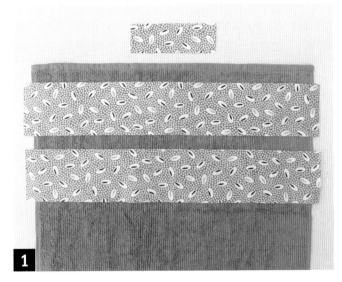

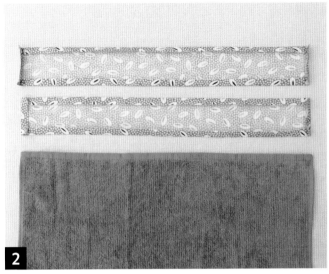

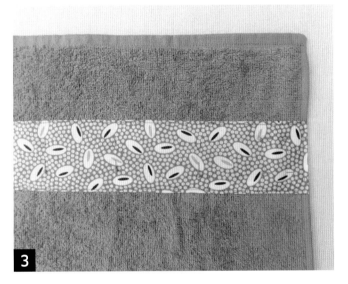

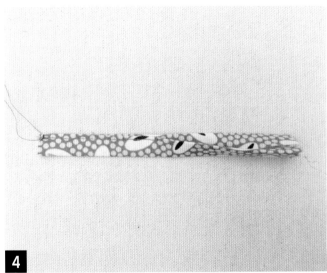

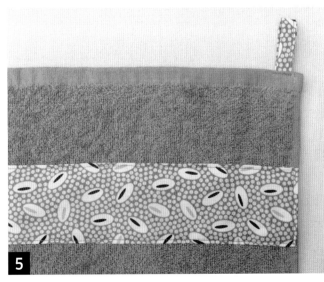

Tip

You could use different fabric remnants to make customized towels for each member of the family.

WASH BAG

This wash bag is extremely practical, with several pockets for storing small items and it folds into a handy shape for packing. It is a more ambitious project than the others in the book, and it combines some of the techniques used in other makes.

Find the templates on pages 136–138

You will need
2 fat quarters of main fabric
1 fat quarter of contrast fabric
30 x 30in (76 x 76cm) of fusible interfacing
Tracing paper or baking parchment
Pencil
Scissors
Tape measure or ruler
Water-erasable pen
Iron and ironing board
Dress-making scissors
Pins
Sewing machine
Thread to match fabric
Sewing needle
9in (23cm) zip
9in (23cm) length of ¼in (6mm)-wide elastic
2 buttons

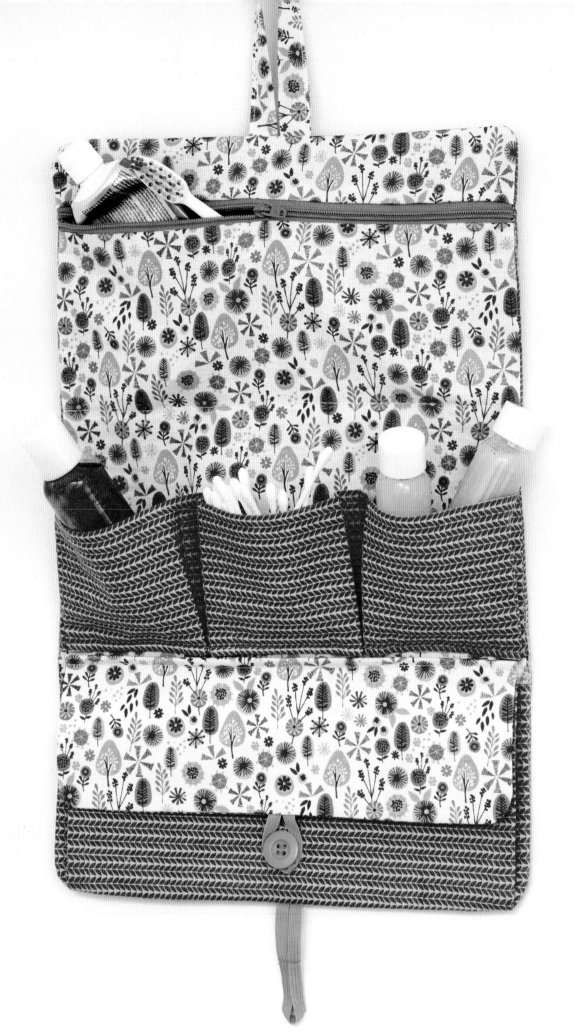

1 Photocopy the templates on pages 136–138 and trace over them onto tracing paper or baking parchment. Cut out with a pair of paper-cutting scissors to make the patterns. Pin the patterns to the fabrics and fusible interfacing, and cut out. Transfer the pattern markings by piercing the tracing paper with scissors and using a water-erasable pen to mark the positions of the dots through the holes. Use a ruler and water-erasable pen to join the lines for the channel markings. Iron the fusible interfacing onto the reverse of the fabric pieces.

2 Take zip bag fabric pieces 1. With the zip facing the contrast fabric, sandwich one side of the zip between the fabrics. Pin and machine sew with a ⅜in (1cm) seam allowance.

3 With the zip facing the contrast fabric, sandwich the other side of the zip between pieces 2 and 3. Stitch it in place with a ⅜in (1cm) seam allowance. See also Zip for a Lined Bag, page 18.

4 Fold back the sandwiched edges of the zip. Stitch the top edge of piece 4 and 1 together with a ¼in (6mm) seam allowance. Join the bottom edge of piece 4 through pieces 3 and 2 with a line of stitching.

5 With right sides facing, fold the central pocket strip (5) in half lengthways and stitch closed along the long side. Turn right sides out and press. With the sewn closed edge facing down, pin both ends of the pocket strip to the sides of the bag (piece 3). Machine sew with a ¼in (6mm) seam allowance. Stitch the pocket along the channel markings. To make the first pocket, press down in the middle of the fabric to create pleats at the sides, and pin pleats in place. Repeat for the remaining pockets. Sew along the bottom of the pockets to secure them.

6 Cut a piece of elastic 3¼in (8.5cm) long and put its ends side by side to make a loop. With the loop facing into the centre of the flap, pin in place. Place the remaining flap piece (7) on top of it, right sides facing. Pin and stitch around the three edges with a ⅜in (1cm) seam allowance, sandwiching the elastic loop. Trim the seams and cut notches on the curves. Turn right sides out and press. Turn the open edge over by ¼in (6mm), pin and stitch in place along the folded edge.

7 To make the lower flapped pocket, with right sides out, fold pocket fabric (6) in half and sew closed along the long edge. Position the pocket on the bag and stitch the sides with a seam allowance of ¼in (6mm). Press in the sides of the pocket to make side pleats and arrange so they are even. Pin and sew along the bottom edge of the bag with a ¼in (6mm) seam allowance.

8 To make the hanging loop, cut a piece of contrast fabric 8 x 2¼in (20 x 6cm), fold it in half lengthways, crease along the fold, then fold in the two sides to meet in the centre so the folded outside edges meet. Pin and sew the sides together (see also Hanging Loop, page 16). Fold the strip in half to make a loop and pin in the centre at the top of the outer fabric. For closing the bag, cut a piece of elastic 5½in (14cm) long, fold it in half to make a loop and pin it in place at the opposite end to the fabric loop.

9 With right sides facing, pin together the outer fabric (piece 8) and lining bag. Stitch around the edge with a ⅜in (1cm) seam allowance, sew curved corners on both the pocket pleats and leave an opening of 4in (10cm) in the side seam. Trim the seam and cut notches on the curved corners. Turn right sides out through the opening in the side seam. Press and hand sew the opening in the seam closed. Add buttons on the pocket of the flapped pocket and on the outside of the bag.

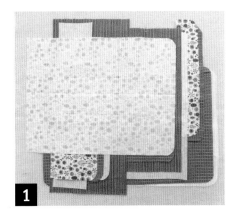

1

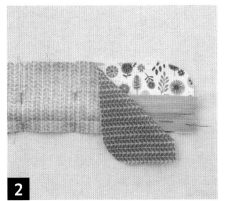

2

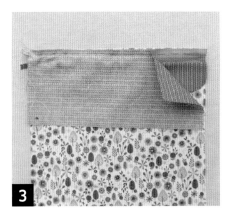

3

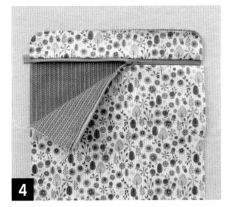

4

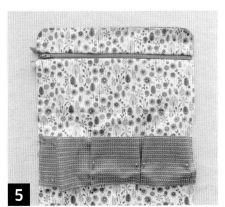

5

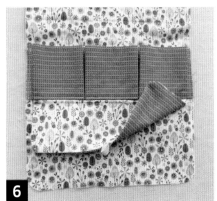

6

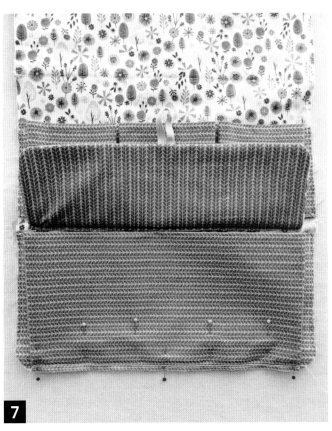

7

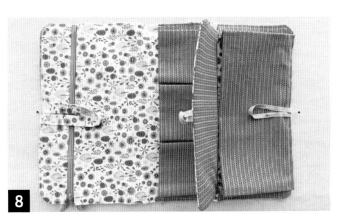

8

9

CUSTOMIZED BATH MAT

This is a cool way of decorating a bath mat and coordinating it with your bathroom. An interesting ampersand design has been used in this project, but you could use any geometric shape. Why not personalize the bath mat by using your initial instead?

Find the template on page 140

You will need
20in (50cm)-wide bathmat
1 fat quarter of fabric for the bath mat edging
1 fat quarter of fabric for the appliqué ampersand
12 x 12in (30 x 30cm) of fusible webbing
Tape measure or ruler
Sewing machine
Thread to match the edging fabric
Sewing needle
Pins
Dress-making scissors
Pen or pencil
Paper scissors
Iron and ironing board

NOTE: Remember that you can piece scraps together with ⅜in (1cm) seams, pressed open, to create strips of fabric to the measurements required.

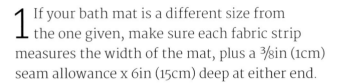
1 If your bath mat is a different size from the one given, make sure each fabric strip measures the width of the mat, plus a ⅜in (1cm) seam allowance x 6in (15cm) deep at either end.

2 Press the fabric strips under by ⅜in (1cm) at each end.

3 With right sides together, pin one strip along one narrow edge of the bath mat. Using a ⅜in (1cm) seam allowance, machine sew the strip to the bath mat with a straight stitch.

4 Fold the strip over the edge of the bath mat and then tuck the raw edge under by ⅜in (1cm). Pin and then hand sew the strip onto the underside of the mat.

5 To make the appliqué, photocopy the template on page 140 and cut it out with paper scissors. Turn the ampersand the wrong way round, pin it onto the backing paper of the fusible webbing and draw around it.

6 Iron the fusible webbing onto the wrong side of the fabric. Cut out the ampersand shape and carefully tear off the backing paper.

7 Iron the ampersand onto the centre of the bath mat. Machine sew around the edge using a zigzag stitch.

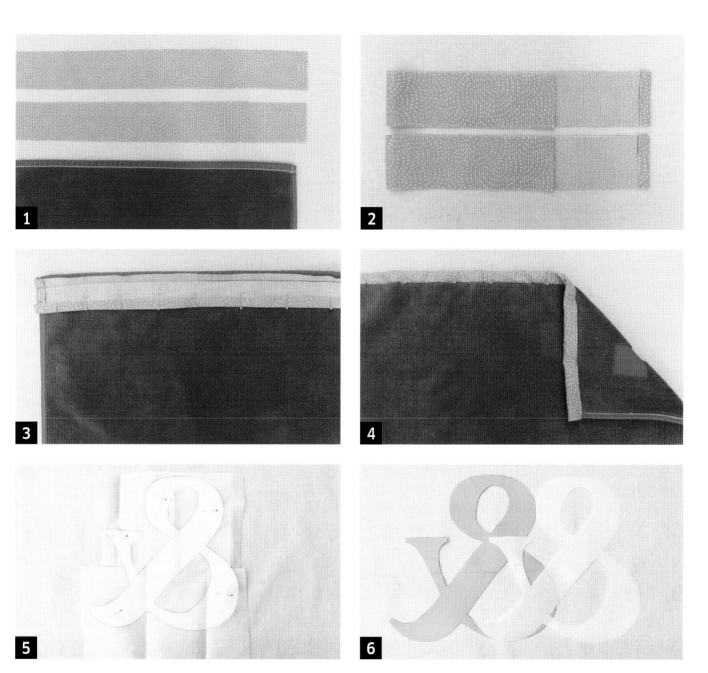

Tip

If you can't find the colour of bathmat you require, you could dye one in the washing machine.

STORAGE BUCKET

You can buy plastic containers for storing bathroom bits and bobs but a fabric bucket is much more attractive and can be made in different sizes. It would also make a handy work basket for all your fabric scraps and sewing paraphernalia.

You will need
1 fat quarter of main fabric
1 fat quarter of contrast fabric
Fusible interfacing: amount depends on size of bucket
Tape measure or ruler
Pencil
Tracing paper or baking parchment
Drawing compass
Scissors
Pins
Dress-making scissors
Iron and ironing board
Sewing needle
Thread to match fabric
Sewing machine

NOTE: One fat quarter will make one large or two small buckets.

1 Draw a circle for the base, using the compass, and draw a rectangle for the sides onto tracing paper or baking parchment and cut out to make patterns. A small bucket needs a base diameter of 5in (12.5cm) and a 8 x 14½in (20 x 36.5cm) rectangle; a large bucket has a base diameter of 7½in (19cm) and a 11 x 21½in (28 x 55cm) rectangle. Seam allowances of ⅜in (1cm) are included. Mark the quarter points on the circle and along the long edge of the rectangle between the seam allowances.

2 Pin the patterns for the bucket sides and bases onto both the main and lining fabrics, mark the seam allowances and the quarter points and cut out.

3 To stiffen the fabric, pin the pieces to the fusible interfacing. Cut out the interfacing and iron it onto the back of all the pieces of fabric to bond.

4 With right sides facing, using a ⅜in (1cm) seam allowance, pin and machine sew the lining to the outer fabric along one long edge.

5 With right sides facing, fold the piece in half so that each side is part outer and part lining. With a ⅜in (1cm) seam allowance, pin and stitch the long side to form a cylinder. Start sewing from the top of the lining, stitch for 1½in (4cm), then leave a 4in (10cm) gap and continue sewing all the way to the end. This is the opening to turn the bucket through when it is completed.

6 Pin the stiffened fabric bases in place, using the quarter points to ensure a neat circle. Sew in place with a ⅜in (1cm) seam allowance. Trim the seams and carefully clip around the circle. See also Fitting a Base to a Cylinder, page 15.

7 Turn the bucket through the open section of side seam. With right sides out, hand sew the side seam opening closed using slip stitch. To form the bucket, push the lining into the outer fabric. Top stitch round the top edge (see page 19).

8 Turn over the top edge to make a cuff of contrasting lining fabric.

Tip

You could make buckets in larger sizes to create storage for other items such as baby clothes or toys.

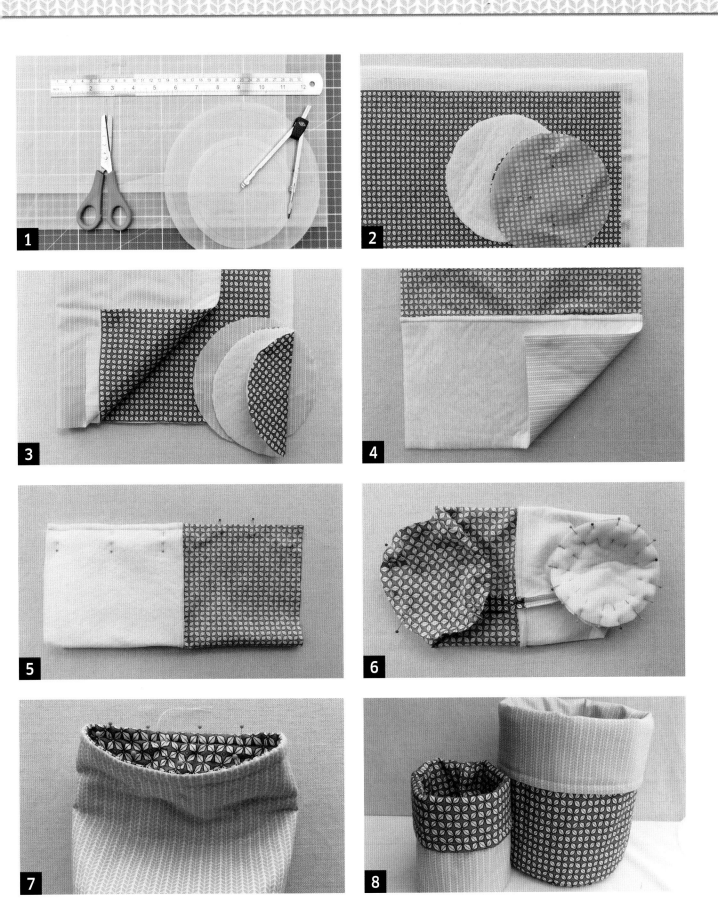

LIVING ROOM

DRINKS COASTER

This project uses a minimal amount of fabric, but if you have plenty of fabric, you could make larger versions as table mats. If you're feeling adventurous, why not make your coasters in star, heart or hexagon shapes?

You will need
6 x 6in (15 x 15cm) of main fabric
6 x 6in (15 x 15cm) of backing fabric
6 x 12in (15 x 30cm) of fusible wadding
Tracing paper or baking parchment
Tape measure or ruler
Drawing compass
Pencil
Scissors
Pins
Sewing machine
Thread to match fabric
Sewing needle
Dress-making scissors
Iron and ironing board

NOTE: One fat quarter will make eight coasters in one fabric.

1 Draw a 5in (12.5cm) circle onto a piece of tracing paper or baking parchment using the drawing compass and pencil. Cut out with a pair of paper-cutting scissors to make a pattern. Pin the pattern onto the main fabric and the backing fabric.

2 Cut out one of each piece from the main and the backing fabrics.

3 Fold the piece of fusible wadding in half, pin the pattern onto it and cut out two circles. Iron onto the reverse of both the main and backing fabrics to stiffen them.

4 With right sides together, pin the two circles together. With a ⅜in (1cm) seam allowance throughout, machine stitch around all the edges, leaving an opening of 1¾in (4.5cm). Clip the edges, then trim the seams.

5 Pull the coaster through the opening so that it is right sides out. Slip stitch the opening closed with a needle and thread.

6 Press and then machine stitch a line of top stitching (see page 19) approximately ¼in (6mm) from the edge to neaten.

Tip

If you don't have a drawing compass, use an upturned glass or mug to make circles. You could use a larger circle to make table mats.

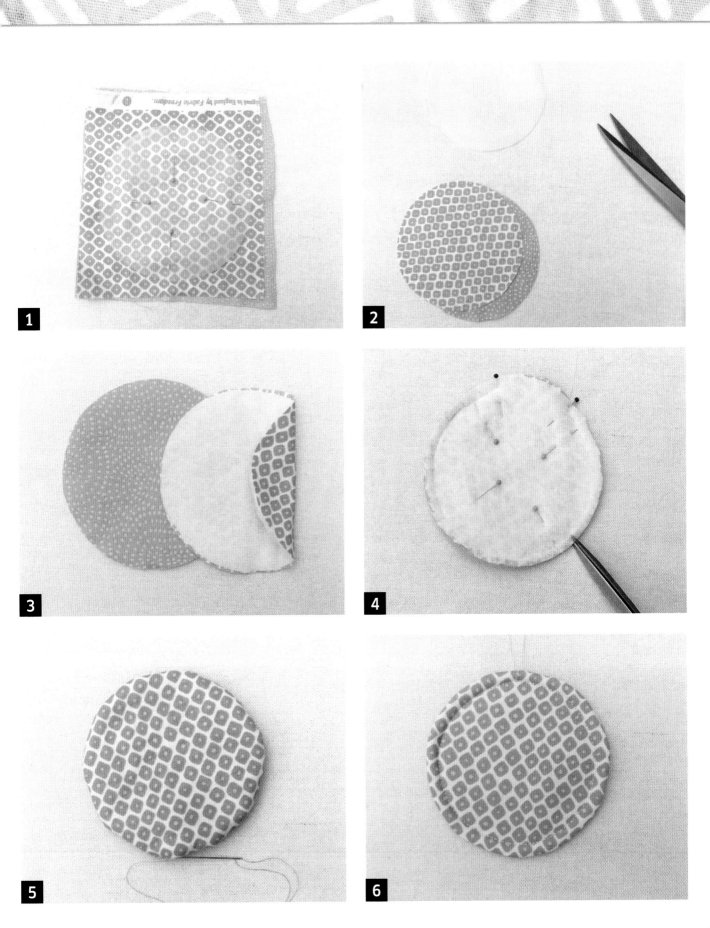

CUSHION COVER

This envelope-back cover is a super easy way to update your cushions. It's all straight seams, you don't have to insert a zip and it's a cinch to slip off the cover for washing. You can even use a less expensive plain fabric or calico for the back.

You will need
3 fat quarters of fabric
Cushion pad, 12 x 12in (30 x 30cm)
Tape measure or ruler
Dress-making scissors
Sewing machine
Thread to match fabric
Sewing needle and contrast thread for tacking
Pins
Iron and ironing board

NOTE: You can sew scraps of fabric together with ⅜in (1cm) seams, pressed open, to make up the pieces for the front and back.

1 From your fabric, cut one piece measuring 14 x 14in (35.5 x 35.5cm) for the front and two pieces measuring 14 x 11in (35.5 x 28cm) for the back. To prepare the back, machine stitch a hem 1in (2.5cm) along one long side of both pieces of fabric – they will overlap when you put the cushion cover together.

2 Pin then tack the two back pieces together, overlapping the hemmed edges so that once tacked together, the back of the cushion cover is the same size as the front fabric.

3 With right sides facing, pin the front and back together. Tack then machine sew along the four sides, leaving a 1¼in (3cm) seam allowance.

4 Remove the tacking, trim the seams and cut the corners. Turn the cover right sides out. Ease the corners out with a pin and press.

5 Insert the cushion pad in the back.

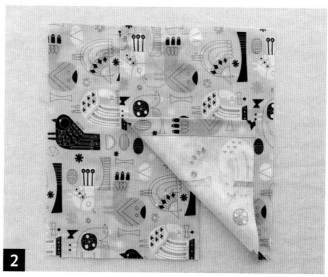

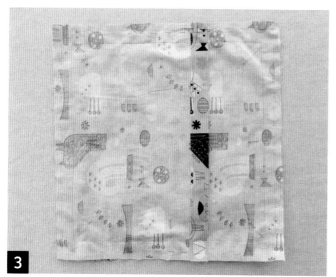

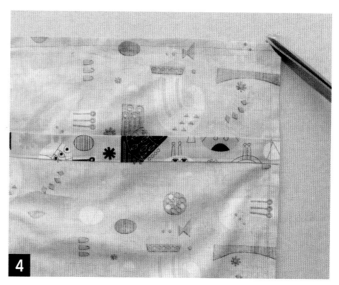

Tip

If you don't have enough fabric for the front and the back, use two different fabrics to make a reversible cushion.

DOOR STOP

This is a great project to use up old rice or any out-of-date pulses. Alternatively, fill it with clean sand or gravel. The pyramid is a neat shape – the door stop is sufficiently heavy to keep a door open but you are unlikely to trip over it.

You will need
1 fat quarter of main fabric
3¼ x 12in (8.5 x 30cm) of contrast fabric for the handle
7¾ x 14¼in (19.5 x 36cm) of fusible interfacing
Tape measure or ruler
Dress-making scissors
Sewing needle
Thread to match fabric
Sewing machine
Pins
1lb (450g) of filling (such as rice, pulses, clean sand or gravel)
Piece of thin card or small piece of paper
Iron and ironing board

NOTE: One fat quarter will make two door stops.

1 With wrong sides facing, fold the handle strip in half lengthways. Press flat. Open up and fold each raw edge to the middle crease just made with the iron. Fold in half again so all the raw edges are hidden. Pin and machine sew close to the edge with a straight stitch. See also Hanging Loop, page 16.

2 Cut a 7¾ x 14¼in (19.5 x 36cm) rectangle from the main fabric. Iron the fusible interfacing onto the reverse of the main fabric to stiffen it.

3 With main fabric right sides facing, fold the fabric so the two short edges meet. Fold the handle in half, and with the loop pointing inwards, sandwich it in one of the seams by the fold (see bottom right of picture). Pin and then machine sew the two side seams. Snip the corners so that when turned through they will make a neater point.

4 Fold out the main fabric shape to bring the two seams to meet. Fold in the bottom corners to meet in the centre. Pin and machine sew the top seam, leaving a 2¼in (6cm) opening for turning.

5 Turn the pyramid shape right sides out. Make a small funnel by rolling a piece of paper or thin card into a cone. Insert the narrow end of the cone into the opening and fill the door stop with your chosen filling.

6 Hand sew the opening closed with a needle and thread.

Tip
You could make smaller pyramids to use as paperweights.

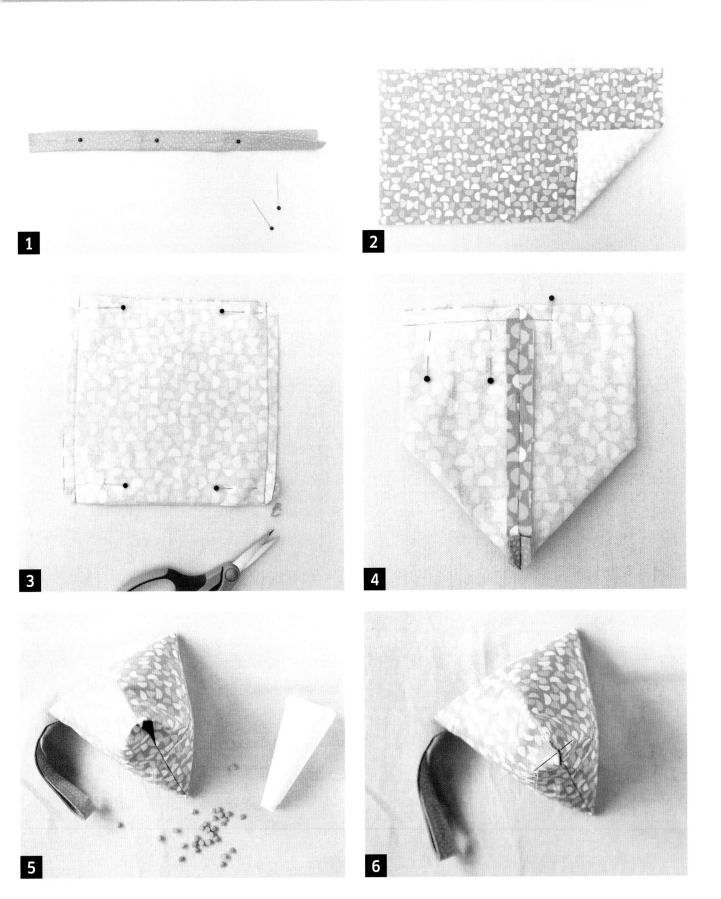

EMBROIDERY-HOOP ART

Embroidery hoops are perfect for making your own eye-catching wall art. A simple design on a contrast fabric is extremely effective and you don't need to be an artist to create it. But do make sure your motif is an appropriate size for the background.

Find the template on page 139

You will need
Embroidery hoop
1 fat quarter of main fabric for background
4 x 6in (10 x 15cm) of plain fabric for motif
Fusible webbing to fit the fabric scrap
Tape measure or ruler
Pencil
Scissors
Iron and ironing board
Dress-making scissors
Sewing machine
Thread in a contrast colour to the motif

1 Cut out the background fabric, making sure it has a diameter 4in (10cm) greater than that of the embroidery frame.

2 Photocopy the template on page 139 and cut out with paper-cutting scissors. Draw around the template onto the paper side of the fusible webbing then iron it onto the reverse of the plain motif fabric.

3 Cut out the motif, then peel off the backing paper. Place the motif onto the right side of the background fabric and iron to bond.

4 Using the contrast-colour thread, top stitch (see page 19) round the edge of the motif.

5 Place the decorated fabric over the inner hoop, press on the outer hoop and tighten the screw.

6 Pull the fabric through to stretch it out neatly and cut off the excess around the edge of the hoop to neaten.

Tip

Before applying fusible webbing to the reverse of the fabric, iron the fabric with a hot iron. This will make the bonding process quicker.

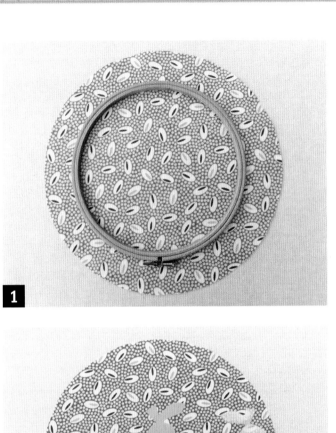

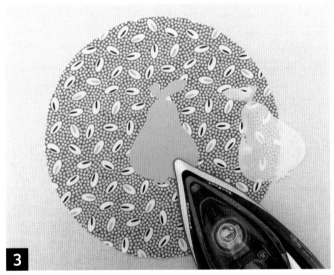

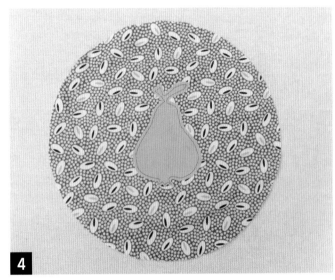

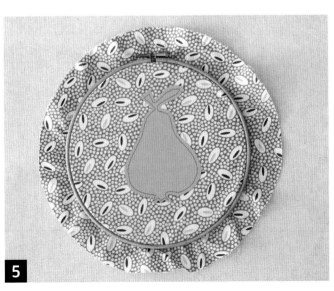

TABLET COVER

It's so much nicer to make your own tablet cover than to buy one. The sizes given here will snugly fit a mini tablet measuring 7¾ x 5¼in (19.5 x 13cm). Check the measurement of your tablet against the measurements given here and adjust as necessary.

You will need
1 fat quarter of main fabric
1 fat quarter of lining fabric
12¼ x 12in (31 x 30cm) of fusible fleece
6½in (16.5cm) length of ¾in (2cm)-wide elastic
Tape measure or ruler
Pins
Dress-making scissors
Sewing machine
Thread to match fabric
Iron and ironing board
Sewing needle

NOTE: You can make the whole project from one fat quarter if you use the same material for the lining.

1 Cut one rectangle measuring 8½ x 6in (21.5 x 15cm) and one rectangle measuring 12¼ x 6in (31 x 15cm) from the main fabric, contrast fabric and fusible fleece. Iron the fusible fleece to the wrong side of the back and front outer fabric pieces. To make the outer cover, cut the elastic to the width of the case and pin it in position on the front section.

2 With right sides facing and the bottom edges lined up, pin the smaller front of the tablet cover onto the back. Machine stitch a ⅜in (1cm) seam down one long edge, across the short edge at the bottom and up the other long edge.

3 Repeat with the lining, leaving a 2¼in (6cm) opening on the lower edge seam for turning the bag later.

4 To make the front cover, fold down the two short front edges by ⅜in (1cm). This is to prevent them being machine sewn when you sew the sides of the flap together. Place the two right sides of the front flaps together. Pin round the three sides of the flap and machine sew with a ⅜in (1cm) seam allowance. Trim the corners.

5 Take the two folded down front edges of the bag, then pin and sew together with a ⅜in (1cm) seam allowance.

6 Turn the cover through the opening in the lining.

7 Press the seams flat and slip stitch the seam opening closed with a needle and thread.

Tip

Use the same technique to make a smaller cover for your phone.

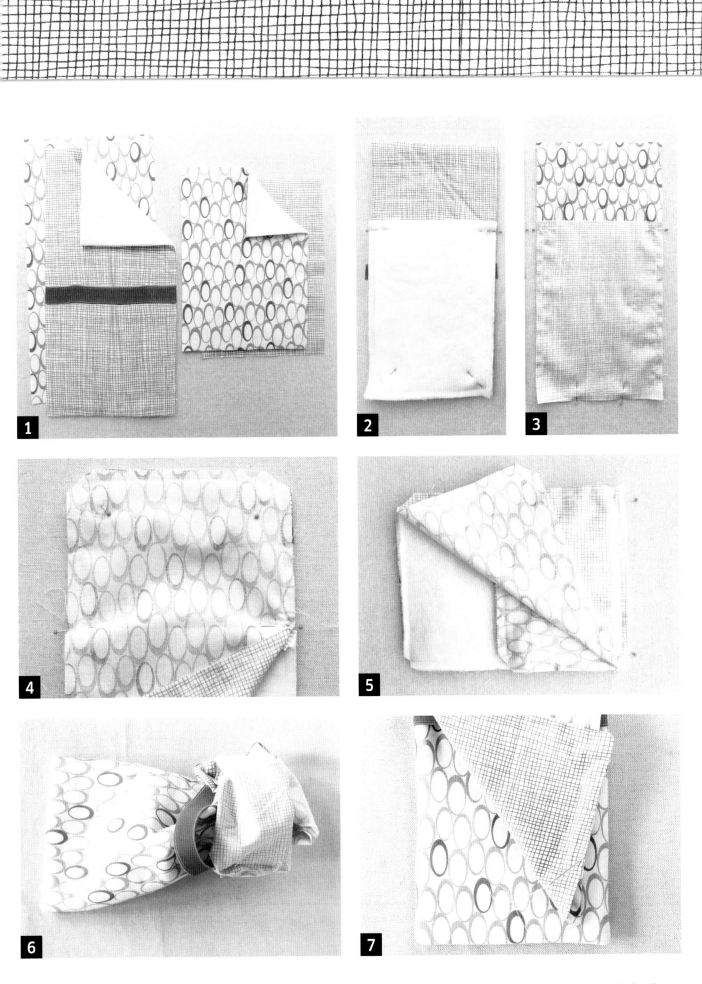

NOTEBOOK COVER

All it takes is a few quick steps to transform an ordinary notebook, elevating it from a mere piece of stationery to a treasured possession. Making a removable cover means you can simply pop a refill in, so that your work can be used again and again.

You will need
To cover an A5 notebook:
1 fat quarter of main fabric
1 fat quarter of lining fabric
16½ x 7in (42 x 18cm) of fusible interfacing
Dress-making scissors
Tape measure or ruler
Pins
Sewing machine
Thread to match fabric
Iron and ironing board
Sewing needle

NOTE: You can make the whole project from one fat quarter if you use the same material for the lining.

1 From the main fabric, lining fabric and fusible interfacing, cut one piece measuring 10½ x 7in (27 x 18cm) and two pieces measuring 3 x 7in (7.5 x 18cm) for the side pockets. Iron the fusible interfacing onto the wrong side of the main fabric for the side pockets and the outer cover.

2 You will make the side pockets first. With right sides facing, machine stitch the lining and main fabric together along one of the long edges using a ⅜in (1cm) seam allowance. Repeat to make the second pocket. Fold open and press along the seam.

3 With right sides facing, pin the pockets to the shorter sides of the main fabric. Machine sew together using a ⅜in (1cm) seam allowance.

4 With right sides facing, pin the lining fabric onto the main fabric and machine stitch together around all sides, using a ⅜in (1cm) seam allowance. Leave a gap of 3in (7.5cm) in the top seam for turning the cover.

5 Trim the seams and snip off the corners to reduce bulk. Turn right sides out through the seam opening.

6 Fold in the edge of the opening, press, and hand sew closed using a needle and thread.

Tip

It's easy to adjust the size for bigger or smaller notebooks – simply measure your notebook from front to back edge, including the spine, and measure the height. Add ¾in (2cm) to each measurement to give you a ⅜in (1cm) seam allowance.

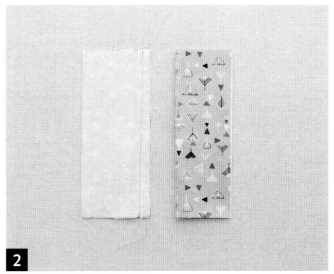

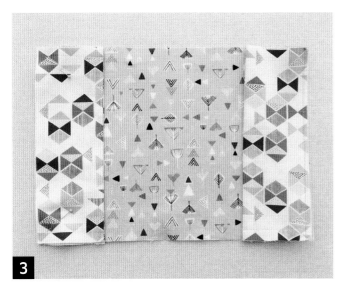

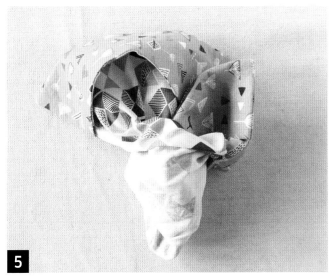

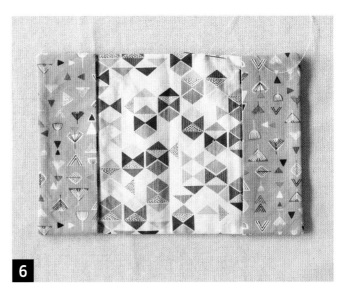

TEMPLATES

Templates that are shown at actual size can be traced
and cut out, or photocopied. For templates that have
been reduced in size, enlarge them on an A3 photocopier
to the percentage stated on the pattern pieces.

TEA COSY
Page 22

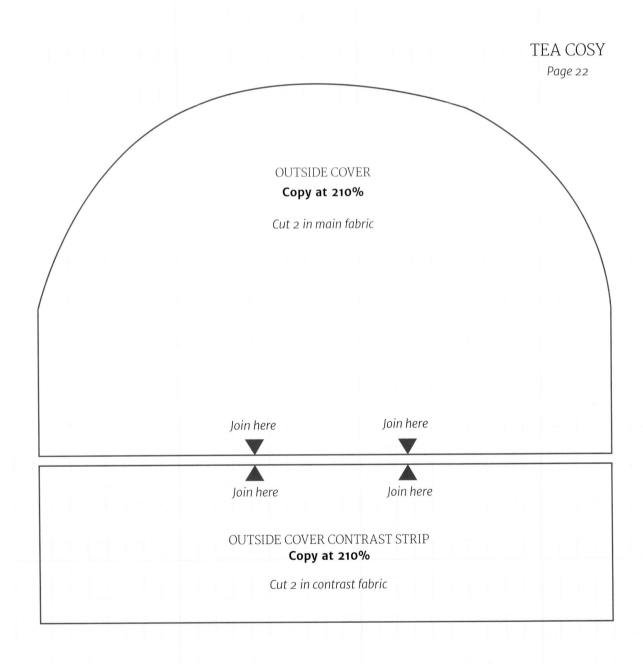

OUTSIDE COVER
Copy at 210%

Cut 2 in main fabric

Join here

Join here

Join here

Join here

OUTSIDE COVER CONTRAST STRIP
Copy at 210%

Cut 2 in contrast fabric

TEA COSY
Page 22

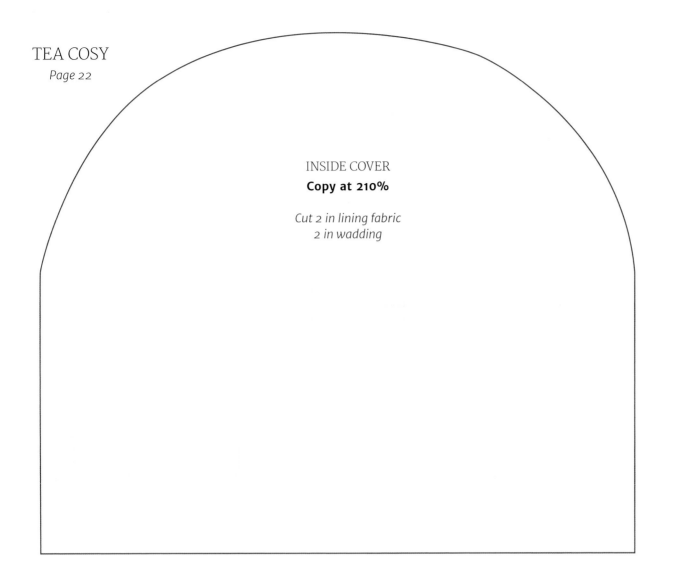

INSIDE COVER
Copy at 210%

*Cut 2 in lining fabric
2 in wadding*

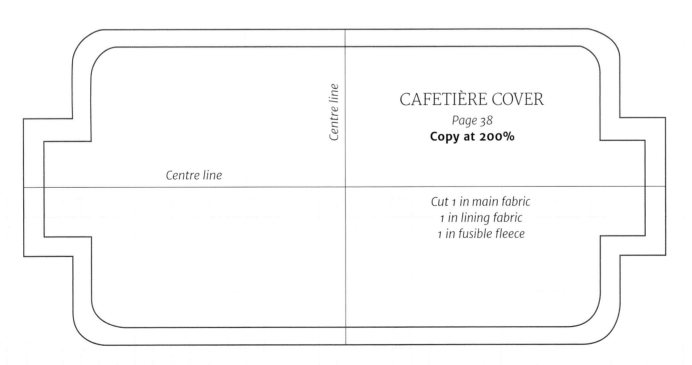

Centre line

CAFETIÈRE COVER
Page 38
Copy at 200%

*Cut 1 in main fabric
1 in lining fabric
1 in fusible fleece*

Centre line

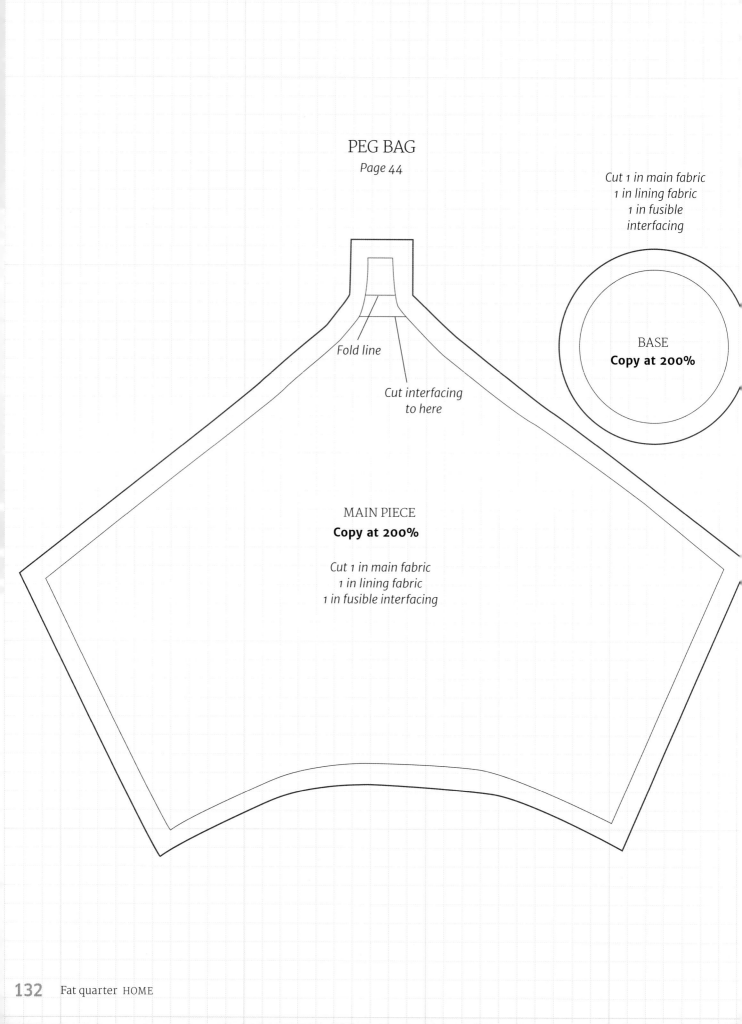

PEG BAG
Page 44

Cut 1 in main fabric
1 in lining fabric
1 in fusible
interfacing

BASE
Copy at 200%

Fold line

*Cut interfacing
to here*

MAIN PIECE
Copy at 200%

*Cut 1 in main fabric
1 in lining fabric
1 in fusible interfacing*

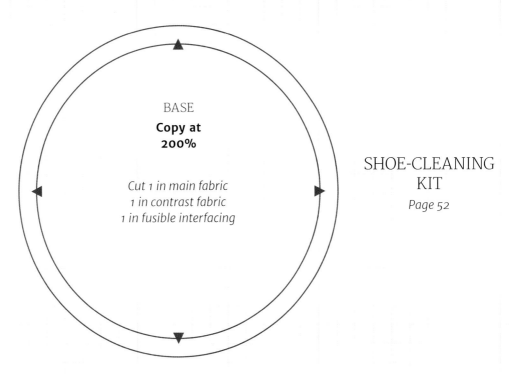

BASE
**Copy at
200%**

Cut 1 in main fabric
1 in contrast fabric
1 in fusible interfacing

SHOE-CLEANING
KIT
Page 52

INNER BAG
(MAIN BODY)
Copy at 400%

*Cut 1 in contrast fabric
1 in fusible interfacing
to halfway mark
(fold line)*

Fold line

side seam

¼ line: match up with base

¼ line: match up with base

¼ line: match up with base

¼ line: match up with base

side seam

EY

Centre of pocket

Quarter point

Channel

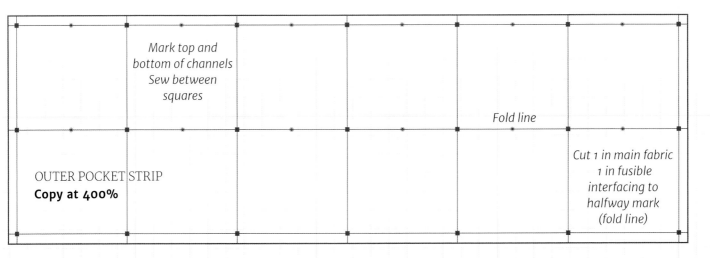

*Mark top and
bottom of channels
Sew between
squares*

Fold line

OUTER POCKET STRIP
Copy at 400%

*Cut 1 in main fabric
1 in fusible
interfacing to
halfway mark
(fold line)*

HOT-WATER BOTTLE
COVER

Page 82

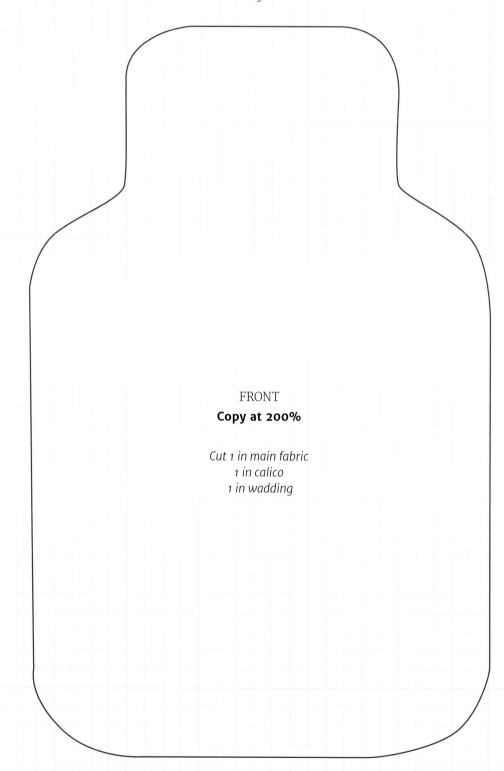

FRONT
Copy at 200%

Cut 1 in main fabric
1 in calico
1 in wadding

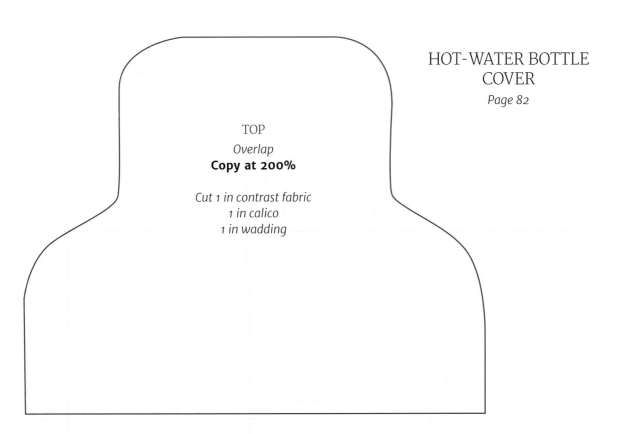

HOT-WATER BOTTLE
COVER
Page 82

TOP

Overlap

Copy at 200%

*Cut 1 in contrast fabric
1 in calico
1 in wadding*

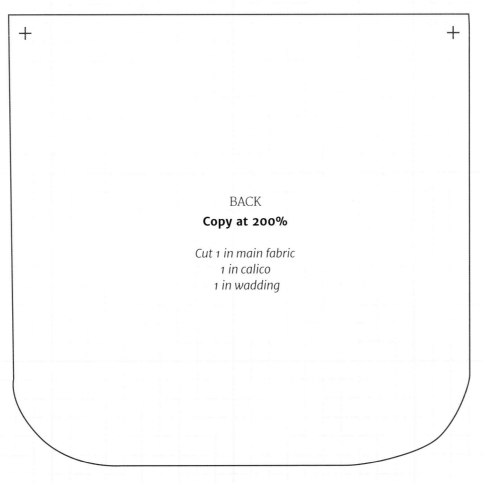

BACK

Copy at 200%

*Cut 1 in main fabric
1 in calico
1 in wadding*

WASH BAG
Page 92

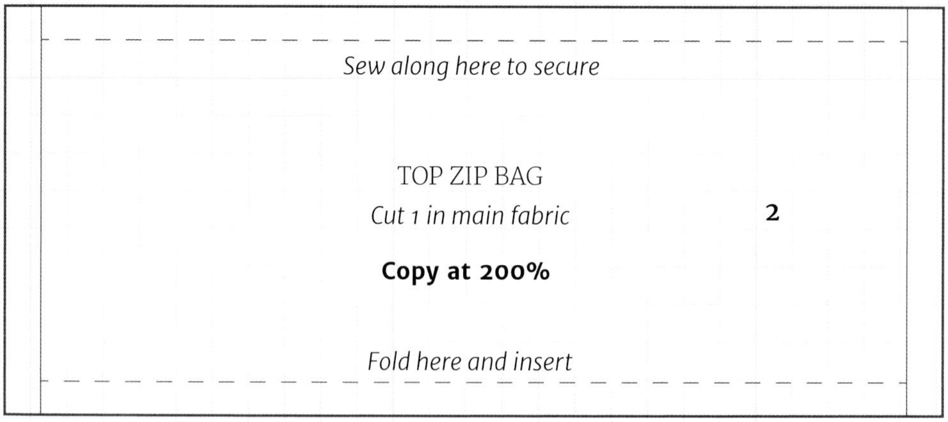

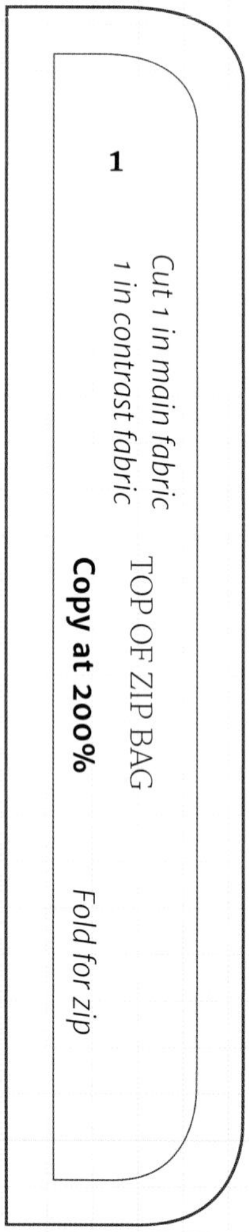

TOP ZIP BAG
Cut 1 in main fabric

Copy at 200%

2

Sew along here to secure

Fold here and insert

1

Cut 1 in main fabric
1 in contrast fabric

TOP OF ZIP BAG

Copy at 200%

Fold for zip

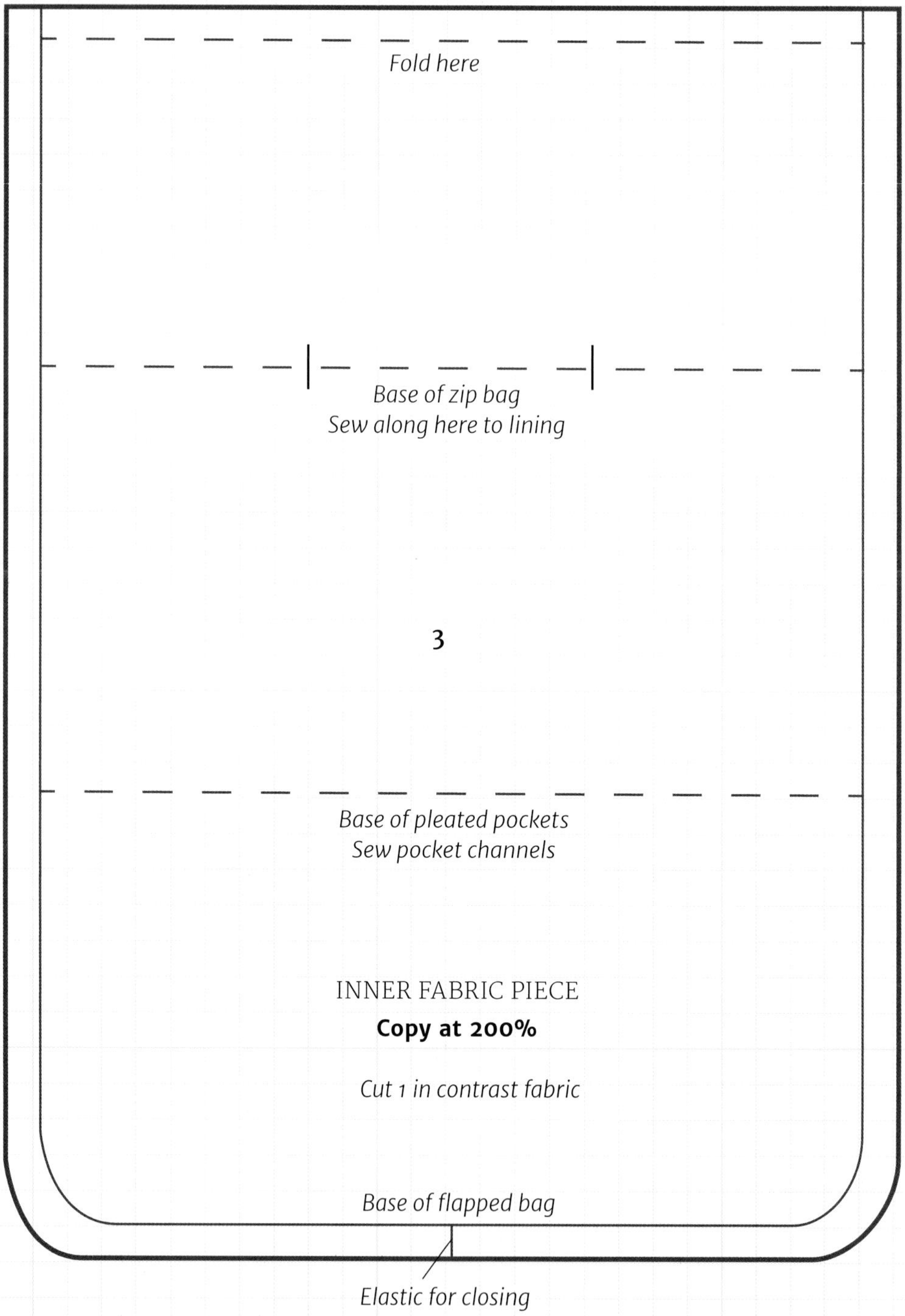

Fold here

Base of zip bag
Sew along here to lining

3

Base of pleated pockets
Sew pocket channels

INNER FABRIC PIECE
Copy at 200%

Cut 1 in contrast fabric

Base of flapped bag

Elastic for closing

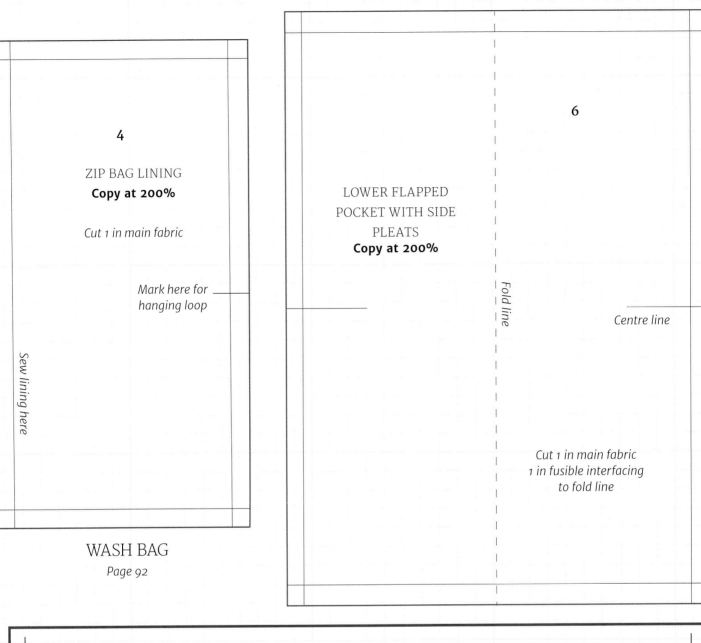

4

ZIP BAG LINING
Copy at 200%

Cut 1 in main fabric

Mark here for
hanging loop

Sew lining here

WASH BAG
Page 92

6

LOWER FLAPPED
POCKET WITH SIDE
PLEATS
Copy at 200%

Fold line

Centre line

*Cut 1 in main fabric
1 in fusible interfacing
to fold line*

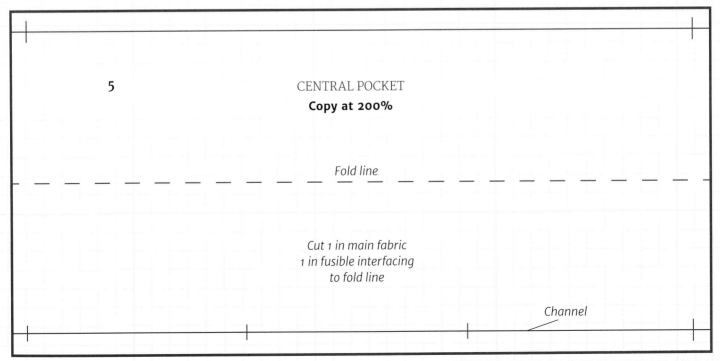

5

CENTRAL POCKET
Copy at 200%

Fold line

*Cut 1 in main fabric
1 in fusible interfacing
to fold line*

Channel

WASH BAG

Page 92

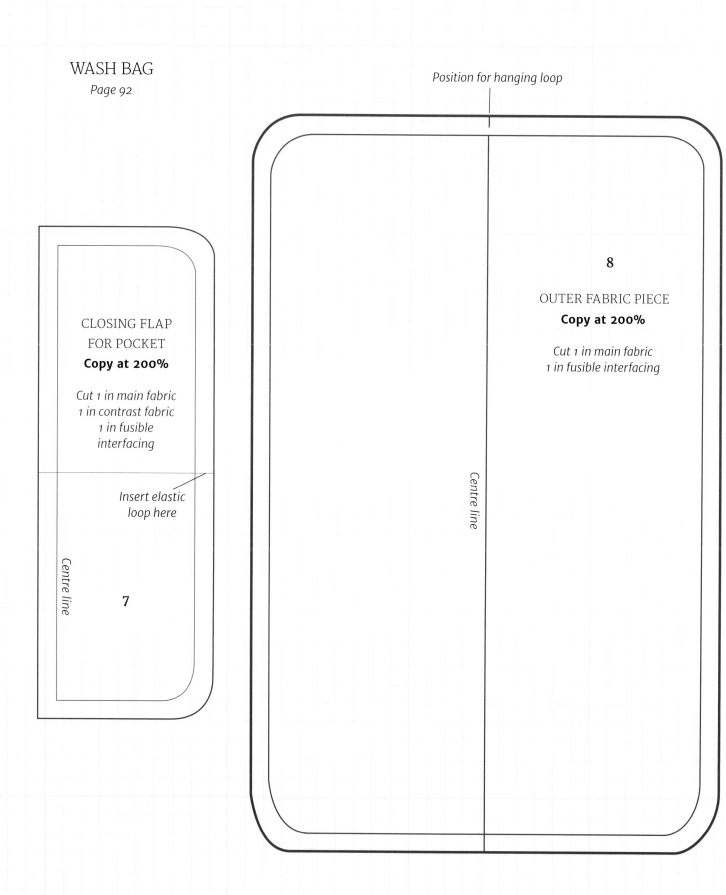

Position for hanging loop

CLOSING FLAP
FOR POCKET
Copy at 200%

*Cut 1 in main fabric
1 in contrast fabric
1 in fusible
interfacing*

*Insert elastic
loop here*

Centre line

7

8

OUTER FABRIC PIECE
Copy at 200%

*Cut 1 in main fabric
1 in fusible interfacing*

Centre line

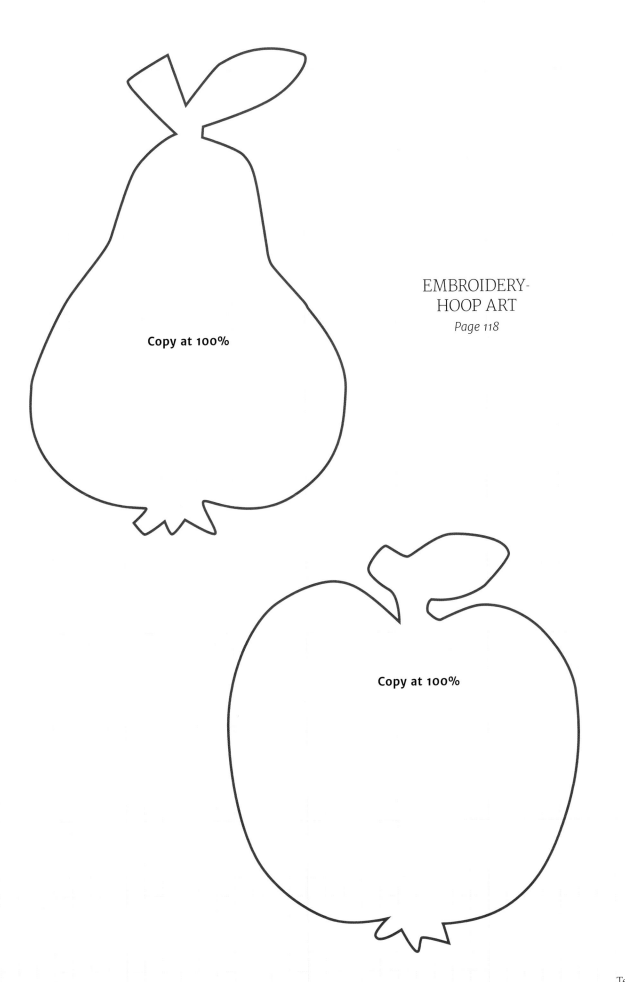

Copy at 100%

EMBROIDERY-
HOOP ART
Page 118

Copy at 100%

CUSTOMIZED
BATH MAT
Page 96

Copy at 200%

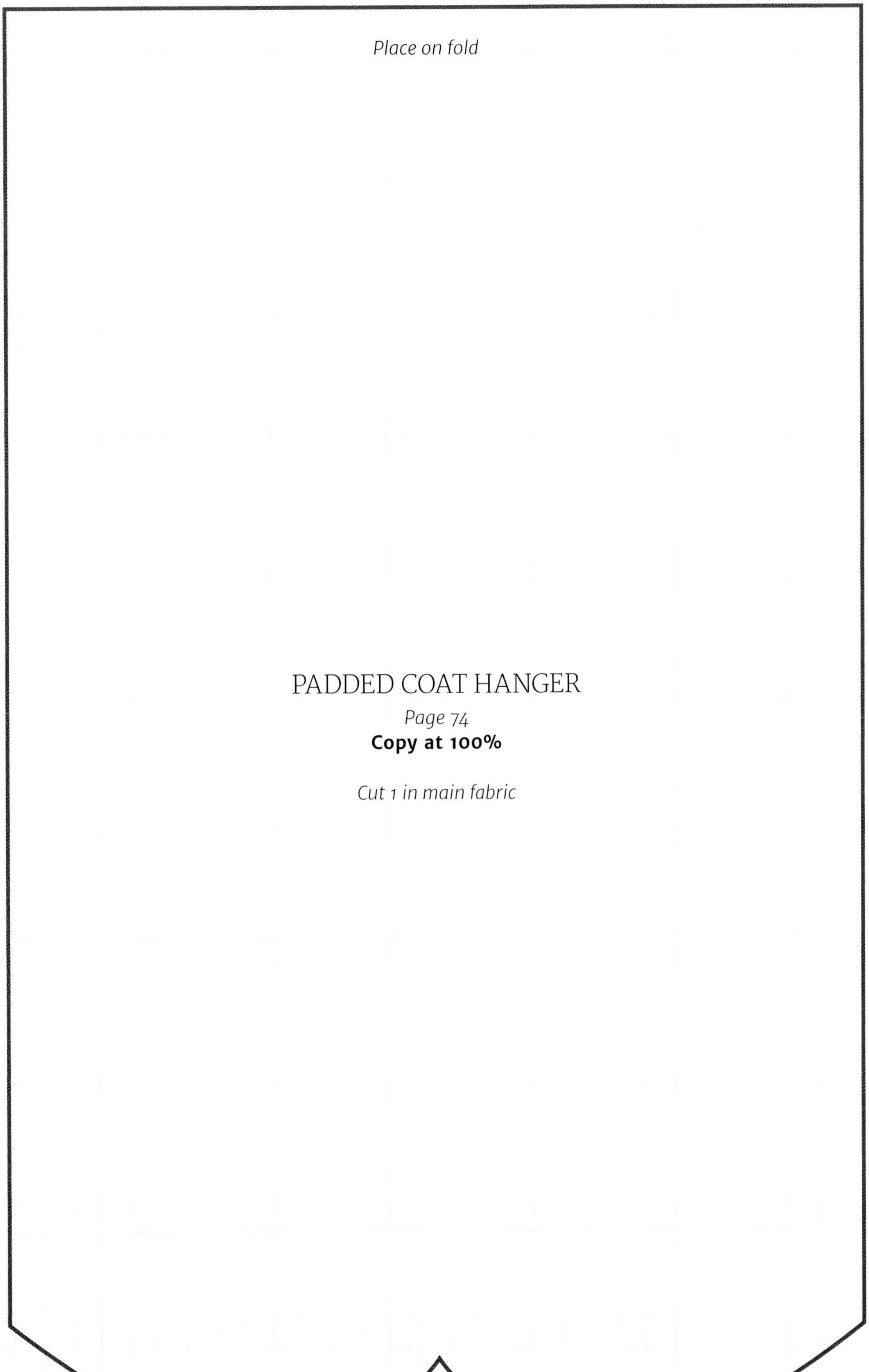

Place on fold

PADDED COAT HANGER

Page 74
Copy at 100%

Cut 1 in main fabric

RESOURCES

Scissors
Fiskars
www.fiskars.co.uk

General haberdashery
Korbond
www.korbond.co.uk

Embroidery floss
DMC
www.dmccreative.co.uk

Fusible webbing, fleece,
interfacing
Vlieseline
www.vlieseline.com

Towels, bath mat, duvet cover
and pillow cases
Ikea
www.ikea.com

Sewing machine
Janome
www.janome.co.uk

ACKNOWLEDGEMENTS

We would love to thank everyone who helped us make this book so beautiful, especially our photographer, the inspirational and generous Rowland, who tirelessly made all our shoots memorable and great fun. Also thank you to Gilda, Sara and Jonathan, the publishing team at GMC Publications, who guided and steered us through this project so professionally.

Our special thanks go to our studio team, supportive as ever, the talented Shaz Collier and Antonia Attwood.

Last but not least, thank you to our wonderful, enthusiastic and patient families, who not only put up with our designing and making and creating a mess, but did so with good humour.

INDEX

To order a book, or to request
a catalogue, contact:

GMC Publications Ltd
Castle Place, 166 High Street,
Lewes, East Sussex,
BN7 1XU
United Kingdom
Tel: +44 (0)1273 488005
www.gmcbooks.com